YOU CHOOSE
BOOKS™

CAN YOU
SURVIVE?

D0096752

CAPSTONE PRESS
a capstone imprint

You Choose Books are published by Capstone Press,
1710 Roe Crest Drive, North Mankato, Minnesota 56003.
www.mycapstone.com

Library of Congress Cataloging-in-Publication Data
Cataloging-in-publication information is on file with the Library of Congress.
ISBN 978-1-51576-198-3 (paperback)

Photo Credits
Alamy: Aflo Foto Agency, 199, Horizons WWP/TRVL, 224, Mary Evans Picture Library, 8, World History Archive, 84; AP Photo: Kyodo News, 193; Bridgeman Images: Private Collection© Look and Learn, Cover Bottom (Titanic), The Illustrated London News Picture Library, London, UK, 71; Capstone Press: 16, Gary Sundermeyer, 295; Dreamstime: Mirella Cosimato, 262, clearviewstock, 274; Getty Images: Bettmann, 31, 143, Corbis Historical, 158, Hulton Collection, 91, 102, Krista Few, 76; Granger, NYC: 10-11; iStockphoto: Ammit, 318, aricvyhmeister, 311, Jim Johnsen, 269, migin, 230, 234, Warwick Lister-Kaye, 246, Skip ODonnell, 213; James P. Rowan: 288, 313; Newscom: EFE/Leo La Valle, 210; Painting © Ken Marschall: Cover Top (Titanic), 14, 23, 37, 46, 60, 67, 105; REUTERS: Jamil Bittar, 284, 316; Shutterstock: 1971yes, 228, Ammit, 304, amybbb, 322, Andrew Bassett, 321, Darrenp, Cover Bottom (Earthquake), 116, Dmitrijs Mihejevs, 258, FloridaStock, 124, Joseph Sohm, 167, 183, kropic1, 154, Kshitij Mishra, 315, MaxFX, 126, Mikadun, 280, mikeledray, 237, oriontrail, 256, pashabo, Design Element, Radu Razvan, 184, Spirit of America, Cover Back Top, 145, Tom Wang, 129, worldswildlifewonders, Cover Bottom (Jaguar); Thinkstock: Moussa81, 273; Wikipedia: Gringer, 118

Printed and bound in the USA.
10267R

TABLE OF CONTENTS

BOOK 1
Can You Survive the Titanic? 4

BOOK 2
Can You Survive an Earthquake? 112

BOOK 3
Can You Survive the Jungle? 220

Author Biographies 327

Can You Survive

THE
TITANIC?

An Interactive Survival Adventure

by Allison Lassieur

Consultant:
Norm Lewis
President, Founder, and CEO
Canadian *Titanic* Society
Simcoe, Ontario

TABLE OF CONTENTS

About Your Adventure...................................... 7

Chapter 1
The Ship of Dreams 9

Chapter 2
Serving and Survival 15

Chapter 3
Save the Family or Yourself?......................47

Chapter 4
Be Prepared and Survive 77

Chapter 5
Why Did Some Survive? 103

Real Survivors 108
Survival Quiz 110

About Your
ADVENTURE

YOU are a passenger on the first voyage of the ocean liner *Titanic*. The ship just hit an iceberg and is beginning to sink. How will you survive?

In this book you'll deal with extreme survival situations. You'll explore how the knowledge you have and the choices you make can mean the difference between life and death.

Chapter One sets the scene. Then you choose which path to read. Follow the directions at the bottom of each page. The choices you make will change your outcome. After you finish one path, go back and read the others for new perspectives and more adventures.

YOU CHOOSE the path
you take through your adventure.

WHITE STAR
LINE

Titanic was as long
as four city blocks.

CHAPTER 1

The Ship of Dreams

It's April 1912. You're thrilled to be traveling on the biggest, most famous ship in the world. The RMS *Titanic* is making her maiden voyage, sailing from England to the United States.

Everything on the ship is better than anything you imagined. Crisp, fresh linens cover the dining room tables, which are set with silver and china. The wood in the magnificent grand staircase gleams. The food is excellent, and there's plenty of it.

Turn the page.

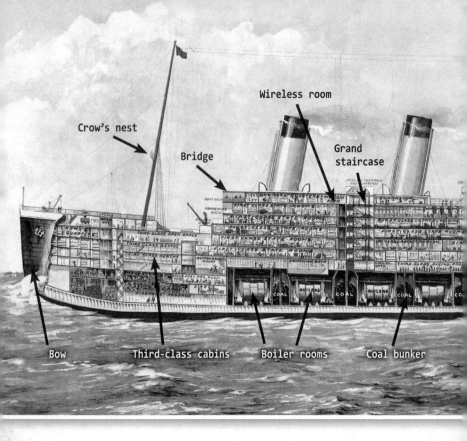

Crow's nest

Bridge

Wireless room

Grand staircase

Bow

Third-class cabins

Boiler rooms

Coal bunker

The ship is also said to be the safest ever built. Its hull is divided into 16 watertight compartments. Devices on the compartment doors will automatically close the doors if water in the compartment reaches a certain height. This feature is designed to keep the water out of the rest of the hull and allow the ship to stay afloat.

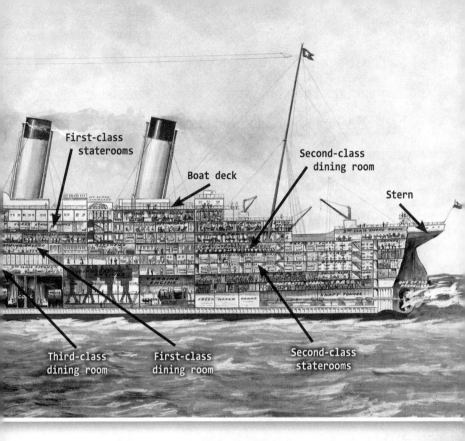

First-class
staterooms

Boat deck

Second-class
dining room

Stern

Third-class
dining room

First-class
dining room

Second-class
staterooms

The only problem you notice is the number of
lifeboats on the deck. There are only 16, plus four
collapsible boats. That's enough boats for about
half of the 2,200 passengers. But there are life vests
in all of the rooms—more than enough for each
passenger and crew member.

Turn the page.

The five-day crossing of the Atlantic Ocean has been smooth. The ship is traveling at an amazing speed of 25 miles per hour. But by Sunday, April 14, you're getting restless. The weather has been good for most of the trip. But this evening, temperatures have dropped below freezing. *Titanic* is scheduled to arrive in New York on Tuesday, April 16. You're ready for this trip to end.

Around 11:40 p.m. Sunday, the huge ship shudders and jerks for a few seconds. Then the gigantic engines fall silent. Stewards appear in the hallways. They urge everyone to put on warm clothing and life vests and go to the upper decks.

Is this a drill? No one seems to know what's going on.

Soon you hear dreadful news. The ship has hit an iceberg. Even then everyone is confident that the ship is only slightly damaged. But what if it isn't? Can you make the right choices to survive?

To be part of the crew as a surgeon's assistant, turn to page **15**.

To experience the sinking as the governess to a wealthy first-class family, turn to page **47**.

To be a 12-year-old boy traveling with your father to New York, turn to page **77**.

Titanic's first-class accommodations were the most luxurious at the time.

CHAPTER 2

Serving and Survival

You stand on the deck of *Titanic* and breathe in the cold night air. It's Sunday, April 14. This is the first time you've had a moment to yourself since the ship left Southampton, England, on April 10. You're one of *Titanic's* medical crew. You are an assistant surgeon to Dr. William O'Loughlin.

When you took the job, you imagined an exciting voyage on the most famous ship in the world. Instead, you've been busy every day tending to the minor hurts and sicknesses of the passengers. You're disappointed that you haven't had more free time. But tonight it seems that everyone is well and safe. You can finally enjoy the amazing ship.

Turn the page.

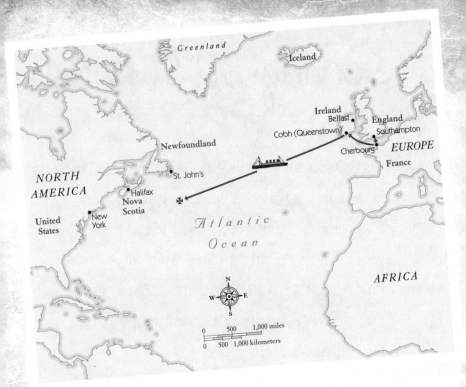

As you look out into the darkness, you think

back to earlier in the evening. You, Dr. O'Loughlin, and several others ate dinner in the first-class dining saloon. You feasted on delicious dishes, such as filet mignon, lamb in mint sauce, roast duckling, and chocolate éclairs. During dinner, everyone talked about how fast the ship was traveling—about 25 miles per hour.

After dinner you wander the decks until around 11 p.m. The weather has turned bitterly cold. You're ready for your warm cabin and bed. You've just fallen asleep when you feel a strange bump. Did the ship hit something? You turn on the light and look at your pocket watch. The time is 11:40 p.m.

Even if the ship has hit something, you're not too concerned. *Titanic* is believed to be unsinkable, after all.

To go back to sleep, turn to page **18**.

To get up to investigate, turn to page **26**.

You turn off the light and drift back to sleep. A loud knock jerks you awake as Dr. O'Loughlin steps in.

"What's happened? What time is it?" you ask.

"It's midnight. The ship has struck an iceberg," he says calmly. "I need you to come with me. Dress warmly and bring your life vest."

You quickly put on your clothes, a wool coat, and a hat. You follow Dr. O'Loughlin to his quarters. The other surgeon's assistants are there with Fourth Officer Joseph Boxhall. Everyone is full of questions.

"Yes, we struck an iceberg," Boxhall says. "The captain sent me down to inspect the damage, but I didn't see anything. Sorry, but I must return to the bridge and give Captain Smith my report." Boxhall disappears. You notice the ship's engines have stopped.

"Gentlemen, I have a bad feeling about this," Dr. O'Loughlin begins. "But our first duty is to the passengers. I'll go to second class to make sure everyone is all right there. I need volunteers to do the same in first class and third class."

To volunteer to go to third class, turn to page **20**.

To volunteer to go to first class, turn to page **25**.

The lower areas of the ship are a maze of narrow hallways and confusing dead ends. But your work has helped you become familiar with the entire ship. You quickly make your way to the third-class lounge. A group of passengers is already there. They look alarmed.

"Doctor, what's happened?" one man asks.

A woman with a baby in her arms says, "I felt a huge bump. Then I heard water rushing in from somewhere."

You tell the passengers what you know. Many of them don't speak English. But you try as best you can to make them understand.

A man comes into the lounge and says, "I heard someone say there's flooding in the boiler rooms. What should we do?"

For the first time you think that the ship is in serious danger. You could brave the bitter cold and go to the deck to find out what is happening. Or you could all stay here in the warmth of the lounge. If the situation is serious, an officer will certainly come and tell you what's going on.

To tell everyone to go up to the deck, turn to page 22.

To advise the passengers to stay put, turn to page 34.

As you start to lead the group out of third class, a crew member appears. You recognize him as John Hart, a steward assigned to this area. "I have orders to send women and children in third class to the boat deck," he says. "I've roused everyone from their cabins. Doctor, help me organize these people. It's a long trip to the deck."

You and Hart take about 30 women and children from the crowd. "The rest of you, wait here," Hart says. "I'll be back."

As he leads the group away, he whispers to you, "These people would never have been able to get out by themselves. Third class is separated from the rest of the ship. There is no direct route to the upper decks." He leads the group on a zigzag route. You walk past the second-class library and down a long hallway past the first-class dining saloon. Then you walk the three flights up the grand staircase to the boat deck.

Passengers who could reach the grand staircase rushed up to the boat deck.

Turn the page.

The boat deck is crowded with people. But no one seems to be in any panic or rush to get into the lifeboats.

Hart helps the shivering third-class women and children into a lifeboat. To Hart's frustration, several of the women jump out of the lifeboat and run inside the warm ship. Finally he shrugs and disappears to get the next group of women and children from third class.

Turn to page 35.

The mood in first class is calm and relaxed. No one seems to realize the danger. You're shocked to see a game of cards going on in the first-class smoking room.

Almost everyone is indoors because it is so cold out on the deck. Several officers are loading people into lifeboats on the boat deck. It's a slow process because no one wants to leave the warmth inside. Many of the boats are launched only half full.

Some people grow bored with waiting and begin to wander back to their rooms. Others urge their families to get into the lifeboats. Your survival instincts tell you that getting into a lifeboat is probably a good idea. Even if this is a false alarm, it's better to be cautious.

Turn to page **35.**

You jump out of bed and get dressed. You don't want to be running around the ship in your nightclothes. Before leaving your room, you grab your life vest.

The hall outside your cabin is quiet and empty. You wonder if you imagined the sound. You see people gathered near the grand staircase. No one seems to be alarmed. Several people are playing cards in the first-class smoking room. One man is hunched over a book. A steward rushes past. You ask him what's going on.

"Nothing to be alarmed about," he replies. "We've struck an iceberg, but it's not serious."

There's some commotion outside on the deck. Part of the deck is covered with chunks of ice. Several young people are playing with them. All that ice on deck makes you nervous, though. You decide to go up to the boat deck. That's where the lifeboats are located.

Once you reach the top of the stairs, you have another decision. Should you go to the port side of the deck or the starboard side? There are lifeboats on both sides.

To go to the port side, turn to page **28**.

To go to the starboard side, turn to page **29**.

There are only a few people on the port side of the deck. But after several minutes, more arrive. Everyone looks as confused as you feel. You spot Second Officer Charles Lightoller and rush up to him.

"Are the lifeboats being launched?" you ask him anxiously.

"Yes, Captain Smith just gave the order," he replies. "But women and children are to be loaded first. I could use your help in loading the passengers."

Turn to page 33.

Not many people are on the starboard side of the deck. But soon the crowd begins to grow. No one seems to know what to do. Just then, First Officer William Murdoch walks up. His face is pale. "The captain's given the order to launch the lifeboats," he tells you. "You had best get in one while you can."

To get into a lifeboat, turn to page 30.

To stay on the ship, turn to page 33.

You help a woman and her teenage daughter into a lifeboat. Then you climb in. Soon all the women and children on the deck near the lifeboat have been loaded, but the boat is not full.

"We can fit more people in here," you call to Murdoch.

"There are no more," he replies. "Launch the lifeboat!"

When the lifeboat is only a few feet above the water, the ropes let go with a jerk. Losing your footing, you teeter and fall over the edge of the boat into the water.

The water is so cold that your brain seems to freeze. Several pairs of hands grab you and haul you back into the lifeboat. Someone throws a woolen blanket over your shoulders.

Many passengers were reluctant to leave the ship for the lifeboats.

"We must get away from the ship," the officer onboard says. "When it sinks, the suction will be so strong that we'll go under the waves with it."

Turn the page.

You're shivering so badly that your hands barely work. But you grab an oar and start to row away from the ship. Several women grab oars as well. It's an oddly calm sight. Orchestra music drifts through the air. All the ship's electric lights are blazing. Everyone on the lifeboat is quiet.

Several women are shaking uncontrollably from the shock and the cold. Most of them only have their nightclothes on beneath their coats and woolen shawls. They probably won't survive this bitter cold for long.

To give your blanket to a passenger, turn to page 38.

To keep it for yourself, turn to page 40.

"Women and children must board the lifeboats!" you shout into the crowd. You grab the arm of the first woman you see.

"No, I won't leave my husband!" she cries, clutching the man next to her.

"You must go," you say, pushing her into the lifeboat. You continue to help several more women and children into the lifeboat until the officer yells, "Launch!" You step away and allow the lifeboat to leave without you.

All the lifeboats are gone. The deck is tilting sharply. Deck chairs, tables, and other objects are rolling down the deck and splashing into the water. Maybe there's still a way to survive, if you can somehow keep out of the water. But if you stay on the ship until it sinks, you're likely to be sucked under the waves with it.

To stay on the ship, turn to page 42.

To risk the water, turn to page 44.

"Don't worry, we'll be fine," you reassure the passengers. But minutes pass, and no officer arrives. Finally you decide it's time to get the passengers to the deck.

You lead the crowd through the halls to the first exit. To your horror, the door to the upper deck is locked! Several men try unsuccessfully to break open the door. The panicked passengers rush back through the passageways. But no one seems to know how to get out of the third-class area.

By now the ship is tilted to one side. As the group turns a corner, a wall of seawater roars toward you. You have no time to react as the wall of water rushes over you. It sweeps you and everyone else in the hall to their deaths.

THE END

To follow another path, turn to page 13.
To read the conclusion, turn to page 103.

You walk toward a lifeboat that's nearly full. "Doctor, get into the boat," an officer calls to you. "These people may need medical treatment for the cold."

You step into the boat, and then it's lowered into the water. You and the other men, including a couple of passengers and an officer, grab oars. When you get some distance away from *Titanic*, you look back. The ship's electric lights are blazing. Orchestra music carries across the water. Few people seem to realize the terrible danger they're in.

Over the next hour, *Titanic* sinks faster. People finally realize the danger, but it's too late. There's nothing anyone in your tiny lifeboat can do but watch in horror as *Titanic*'s stern rises higher and higher. Finally the mighty ship breaks in two and falls with a crash. Hundreds of people are thrown into the water.

Turn the page.

You know people can last only a few minutes in such cold water before dying of hypothermia. Sure enough, in less than an hour the screams and moans grow quiet.

You spend the night keeping the other survivors warm. You try not to think about the bodies floating in the icy water just a few feet from the boat.

About 3:30 a.m., the rescue ship *Carpathia* appears on the horizon. Tears of relief fill your eyes as you help the people in your boat board the rescue ship. You're grateful that you all survived, but sad that so many died.

People watched in horror from the lifeboats as *Titanic* went down.

THE END

To follow another path, turn to page 13.
To read the conclusion, turn to page 103.

"Here," you say, draping the blanket over the shoulders of one of the women. The cold air hits you like a slap.

"God bless you, sir," she says through her chattering teeth.

"The most important thing for us right now is to stay as warm as possible," you say to the other passengers. Soon everyone is stomping their feet and rubbing their hands.

Everyone in the lifeboat stares in shock as the stern of *Titanic* rises higher and higher. Hundreds of passengers fall, are thrown, or jump into the freezing black water. The music stops and the electric lights go out for good as *Titanic* pauses, groans, and plunges into the water. The air is filled with the screams of people in the water, begging to be rescued.

"We should go back to get some survivors," you say to the officer. "There's plenty of room in the lifeboat."

"No!" the officer snaps. "If we go back, they will overtake us and cause the boat to capsize. We'll all die."

Finally the sea is silent. You're still wet and shivering. Soon you start to feel sleepy. "I'll just rest a few minutes," you think as you sink to the bottom of the lifeboat. You don't realize that you're suffering from hypothermia. When you close your eyes, it's for the last time.

THE END

To follow another path, turn to page 13.
To read the conclusion, turn to page 103.

You feel ashamed, but you know that using the blanket to stay warm is your best chance for survival. Instead you put your arm around the woman next to you. The two of you huddle together for warmth.

Just beyond the lifeboat, *Titanic* is sinking faster. The ship's stern rises higher and higher out of the water, until its huge propellers are lifted above the waves. Screaming passengers slide down the deck into the water. Others jump. Still more brace themselves against the railing.

One of the huge smokestacks tears apart from the ship and falls to the water with an enormous crash. A few moments later *Titanic* disappears beneath the waves for good. You look away, tears in your eyes.

You know you're lucky to have survived the disaster. Your decision to keep your blanket helped. You and the others on the boat are cold but all alive when the ship *Carpathia* arrives around 3:30 a.m. It's a sight you'll remember for the rest of your life.

THE END

To follow another path, turn to page 13.
To read the conclusion, turn to page 103.

As the ship's stern rises higher, you wrap your arms and legs around the metal rails and hang on. You hear several explosions as the ship slides into the water with alarming speed. You take several deep breaths. Then you jump as far out and away from the sinking ship as you can.

The cold water feels like knives as you are pulled under by the suction of the ship. As hard as you kick, you seem to be going deeper. With a desperate burst of energy, you kick free of the whirling current. You pop out of the water, gasping and coughing, but alive.

Hundreds of people are in the water, frantically splashing and crying, "Help me!" "Save us!" You know that no one is coming to save you. What you must do now is get out of the water. Your chances of dying from hypothermia are much greater in the freezing water.

You spy a wooden table floating nearby and climb onto it. You slowly paddle away, hoping to get clear of the wreckage. Suddenly the table tips and hits you in the head. You're flung back into the water. Unconscious, you float in the water until your frozen body sinks to the bottom of the ocean.

THE END

To follow another path, turn to page 13.
To read the conclusion, turn to page 103.

Holding your breath, you leap as far out into the ocean as you can. The freezing water feels like knives cutting your skin. The water is already filled with hundreds of people screaming for rescue.

You've got to get out of the water before you die of hypothermia. You start swimming. Wreckage is everywhere, but there isn't anything big enough for you to float on. Then you spy a strange sight. About 30 men are standing atop an overturned boat. One of them is Second Officer Charles Lightoller. You swim to the boat and climb aboard.

"We have to stay afloat," Lightoller says. "Everyone stand in two rows along the boat. When a wave rolls us, we can stabilize ourselves."

Through the night you stand with the other men, following Lightoller's orders to "Lean to the left!" "Stand upright!" "Lean to the right!" to keep the upturned boat afloat.

Soon your wet, frostbitten feet go numb, but you keep standing. Several men collapse and disappear into the water. But you're still standing when the lights of the ship *Carpathia* appear. "We've made it," you whisper hoarsely. Staying awake helped you survive the wreck of *Titanic*.

THE END

To follow another path, turn to page 13.
To read the conclusion, turn to page 103.

First-class passengers swept down the grand staircase on their way to dinner.

CHAPTER 3

Save the Family or Yourself?

You look around at the elegance of *Titanic*'s first-class rooms. You can't believe your good fortune. When you answered the newspaper ad for a governess, you never imagined you'd be traveling on the "Ship of Dreams."

Edward and Annabelle Charles hired you to look after their three children on the voyage. The children are 2-year-old Henry, 6-year-old Agnes, and 12-year-old James. You and the children have spent most of the voyage exploring the ship. It's been great fun.

It's Sunday night, April 14, and you've tucked the children into bed and told them a story. They love your stories about how your brothers helped build this grand ship. Once the children are asleep, you turn off the lamps and go into the main sitting area. Mrs. Charles is there, reading.

"The children are in bed, ma'am," you say.

"Thank you," Mrs. Charles says, smiling. "Why don't you get yourself some dinner? I believe the valets' and maids' dining saloon is still open."

Titanic has a separate dining room for the servants of its wealthy passengers. When you arrive, several servants are eating a late supper. One of them is Rosalie Bidois, Madeleine Astor's maid. Next to Rosalie is Emilie Kreuchen, maid to Elisabeth Walton Robert. Soon you're laughing and talking together.

"I hear the ship is going faster than any other ship!" Emilie exclaims. "We'll surely be in New York before Tuesday."

After the meal you walk about the ship until around 11:30 p.m. By now the weather has turned very cold. You should be getting back. Just as you get to the first-class cabin, the ship jerks slightly. It doesn't feel like much, but it is unusual.

To go into the cabin, turn to page 50.

To return to the decks, turn to page 52.

You forget the slight bump as soon as you get inside the warm cabin. You check on the children. Then you go to your room, a small cabin adjoining the main cabin. Soon you're asleep.

Sometime later a noise awakens you. Something's wrong. The ship's engines have stopped. Mrs. Charles and the children are huddled in the main cabin. Mrs. Charles says, "The steward has ordered us to put on our life vests and get to the boat deck immediately."

"But there's no danger," James says. "Papa said so before he left!"

You nod, trying to look braver than you feel. "Remember what my brothers told me. *Titanic*'s got a one-inch-thick hull and 16 watertight compartments. There's no way it can sink. But let's put on as many warm clothes as we have and do what the steward says, just in case."

"I hate those scratchy wool stockings!" Agnes whines. You put several layers on baby Henry. James is already dressed.

"Wait, I can't leave without my things!" Mrs. Charles cries as she rummages through the luggage, pulling out photos, jewelry, and other personal items.

"We don't have time," you tell her, a hint of panic in your voice.

"I'll only be a moment," she says. "Take the children—I'll be right behind you."

To take the children to the boat deck, turn to page **59**.

To wait for Mrs. Charles, turn to page **62**.

Your brothers taught you to trust your instincts on a ship. The bump seemed to be from the front of the ship, so you start walking in that direction. You ask the first steward you see what's going on.

"Nothing wrong, ma'am," he says. "Probably dropped a propeller or something." Just as you get ready to return to your room, you spy Emilie. She looks worried.

"We've hit an iceberg," she whispers. "They say we hit up in the front of the ship."

"Let's go see," you say. You're almost to the front of the ship when you realize that the ship's engines have stopped. That's not a good sign. Maybe something has happened to the boilers. "I know where the boiler rooms are," you say. "Follow me!"

You know passengers aren't allowed below decks. But this is an emergency. You and Emilie race down several sets of stairs and passageways toward the bottom of the ship. In the mail room, several postal workers are in knee-deep water. They are scrambling to save bags of mail.

"This is serious," Emilie says. "What do we do?"

The best way to survive a disaster at sea is to get into lifeboats as fast as possible. But maybe the damage isn't as bad as it looks.

To try to find out more, turn to page 54.

To wake the Charles family, turn to page 56.

"I'm not going to wake Mr. and Mrs. Charles unless I'm sure we're in danger," you tell Emilie as you return to the upper deck. "This ship has a one-inch-thick hull and 16 watertight compartments. It's made to withstand a collision like this."

You see one of *Titanic*'s stewardesses, Mary Sloan, speaking to a tall gentleman.

"That's Thomas Andrews," Emilie says, pointing to the man. "He helped design and build *Titanic*."

As you approach Mary and Mr. Andrews, you overhear their conversation.

"Sir, is the ship really in danger?" Mary asks.

"It is very serious, but keep the bad news quiet for fear of panic," Andrews replies. He quickly strides away. Mary disappears as well.

Emilie looks at you in horror. "I must warn Mrs. Robert immediately!" She runs down the hall.

You have to warn the Charles family. Several stewards and stewardesses are knocking on passengers' cabin doors. Many people are angry at being awakened. Some slam their doors and go back to sleep. Others obey orders and put on life vests. No one seems as panicked as you feel.

You start down a flight of stairs and stop abruptly. The bottom step is underwater. The Charles' cabin is not far. What if they're trapped inside?

To try to get to the cabin, turn to page 65.

To go back up to the deck, turn to page 66.

"It's better to be safe than sorry," you think as you go back to the cabin. You tell Mr. and Mrs. Charles what you saw in the mail room.

Mr. Charles looks worried. "Let me talk to the captain," he says. He strides out. When Mr. Charles returns, he looks grim. "We've struck an iceberg," he says. "Let's get the children to the lifeboats." You and Mrs. Charles quickly bundle the children in as many warm layers as you can find. You put on two layers of stockings and an extra sweater under your overcoat.

There's an odd sense of calm on the boat deck when you and the family arrive. A few of the lifeboats have already been launched, but most of them were only half full. No one wants to get into a lifeboat when they can stay warm and dry on the ship.

"You must get in," Mr. Charles says, pushing Mrs. Charles toward the nearest lifeboat. Suddenly the sky is filled with a shower of white stars. Captain Smith has sent out a distress signal. The situation is worse than you thought.

The calm mood turns to panic as people realize the danger. The crowd surges around you, pulling Agnes' hand from your grasp. Frantically you push forward, looking for anyone in the family. But there are too many people! You're holding baby Henry, who starts to cry.

To try to find the family, turn to page 58.

To get into a lifeboat, turn to page 69.

Breaking free of the panicked crowd, you frantically search for the Charles family. By now people are fighting to get in the lifeboats. Several men try to jump into boats, but the officers pull them out.

You see Mr. Charles' black hat above the crowd near the lifeboats on the other side of the ship. With relief you run to him.

"You must get in," Mr. Charles tells his wife. "The lifeboats are almost filled. You don't have much time."

"I'm not going without you!" Mrs. Charles cries.

"Then let the governess take the children into a boat," Mr. Charles says gently.

"No, I will not be separated from the children!" Mrs. Charles is almost hysterical. "We're going back inside where it's warm and dry."

To try to save the children, turn to page 71.

To obey Mrs. Charles, turn to page 73.

You carry Henry and lead the other children to the boat deck. The deck is crowded with confused passengers. Officers are shouting orders. The ship seems to be tilting. There is no sign of Mr. or Mrs. Charles.

"Women and children!" shouts an officer. He sees you and the children. "You there, into the lifeboat!"

"But their mother isn't here!" you cry. "We must wait for her!"

"Get in," a familiar voice says in your ear. Mr. Charles is standing behind you with a grim expression on his face. "I'll see to it Mrs. Charles gets into a lifeboat."

Mr. Charles and the officer help you and the children into the lifeboat. "Papa!" Agnes screams.

Turn the page.

"Don't worry," Mr. Charles says, smiling. "Mama and Papa will see you very soon." Agnes buries her head in your lap as the lifeboat is lowered into the water. The two *Titanic* officers aboard row away from the sinking ship.

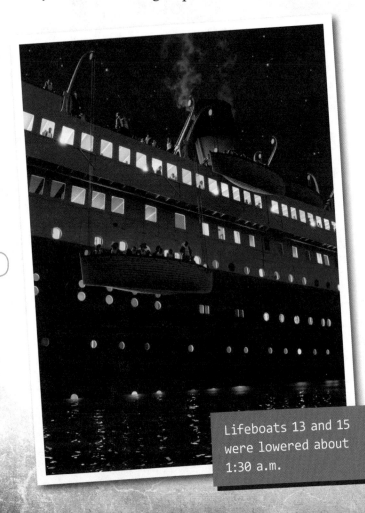

Lifeboats 13 and 15 were lowered about 1:30 a.m.

Before long, *Titanic*'s stern rises high into the air. People onboard are thrown into the freezing ocean. You coax the children into singing songs. You hope it will distract them from the terrible screams of the dying passengers. Soon the ship slips below the surface of the sea.

Once the sea is quiet, the children sob themselves to sleep. The night seems to last forever, but the sky gradually begins to brighten. One of the people on the lifeboat gives a shout. A rescue ship is coming!

You don't know if you'll ever see Mr. and Mrs. Charles again, but at least you and the children have survived.

THE END

To follow another path, turn to page 13.
To read the conclusion, turn to page 103.

Mrs. Charles seems to take forever to pack. She tucks the photos and jewelry into a bag. Then she pulls a wad of cash from the safe. "Let's go," she says finally. The small clock on the table reads 1:30 a.m.

"Where's Mr. Charles?" you ask.

"We'll meet him on deck," Mrs. Charles replies. You lead her and the children down the hall toward the main elevator.

"Look," James says, pointing to the end of the hallway. Water is rushing toward the group.

"Follow me," you say, turning around. "I know a different way."

Your brothers spent months working on *Titanic*. They told you about every passageway and ladder in the ship. You herd the family back down the hall as fast as you can. Water laps right behind you.

You run through several more hallways and up a flight of stairs. Finally you reach the aft first-class staircase. With relief you stumble onto the boat deck.

"Where are the lifeboats?" you ask an officer.

"All gone here," he says. "Try the port side of the deck, but be quick."

It's all you can do to drag the children and Mrs. Charles to the port side of the ship. A few boats there are still being loaded. Someone picks you up and throws you and Henry into a lifeboat, along with Mrs. Charles and Agnes. They leave James on deck.

"James must come with me!" Mrs. Charles screams. "He's just a child!"

"No men or big boys," the officer says. Mrs. Charles begins to cry.

Turn the page.

"Jump, James!" you yell, holding out your arms. Before the officer can stop him, James leaps off the deck and into the lifeboat. When the boat reaches the water, two crew members onboard grab oars and start rowing. You're a safe distance from the ship when it slips under the water. You're happy when you are rescued about two hours later.

But you are heartbroken to learn that Mr. Charles went down with the ship.

THE END

To follow another path, turn to page 13.
To read the conclusion, turn to page 103.

The idea of the children being trapped is too much for you to bear. You jump into the water and wade down the hall to the cabin. The door is open, and the cabin is flooded. The Charles' beautiful things are floating everywhere. But thankfully the family is gone.

By now the water is hip-deep. You have trouble getting out of the cabin. If you can make it to the stairs, you'll surely survive. Just as you get there, a wave of water rolls down the hallway. It lifts you off your feet and carries you forward. Something hits your head. You fall unconscious, drowning below decks as *Titanic* sinks.

THE END

To follow another path, turn to page 13.
To read the conclusion, turn to page 103.

When you reach the deck, you scan the crowd for Mrs. Charles and the children. But you don't see them. Officers stand near each lifeboat. They help women and children get in the boats and keep men and older boys away. As you debate which way to go next, James appears in the crowd.

"Blessed be!" you cry, hugging him tightly. "Where's everyone else?"

"Mama and the girls got on a lifeboat," James says, trying not to cry. "They wouldn't let me on because I'm a big boy. I can't find Papa."

You swallow hard. "Let's get on one of these lifeboats, shall we?" you say. "But we'll have to play a little trick on the officers, all right?"

James nods and wipes his eyes. You wrap your shawl tightly around James' head and shoulders, hiding his short hair. Then you push through the crowd to the nearest lifeboat.

"Please let me and my sister on this boat!" you cry to the officer in charge. He barely looks at James as he lifts him up and tosses him gently into the half-full lifeboat. You climb in after James.

As the boat is being lowered, the sky explodes with a bright flash and a loud hiss. "That's a distress signal," you tell James. "We got off *Titanic* just in time."

Titanic's distress signals looked like a fireworks display.

Turn the page.

Several passengers grab oars and start to row away from the ship. Terrible sounds of screaming and tearing metal fill the air, but you can't look. After what seems like forever, everything is quiet.

About 3:30 a.m. a ship named *Carpathia* sails into view. One by one the survivors are lifted onto the ship. Suddenly James shouts, "Mama!" Mrs. Charles has Henry in her arms and is holding Agnes' hand. "Is Mr. Charles here too?" you ask. Mrs. Charles shakes her head sadly. You're grateful that you all survived, but everyone is saddened because Mr. Charles did not.

THE END

To follow another path, turn to page 13.
To read the conclusion, turn to page 103.

"Here, miss," a stranger says, leading you by the arm to a lifeboat. "There's room for you and your baby here."

"Please, sir, the rest of the family is here somewhere!" you cry as the stranger lifts you into the lifeboat. He pats Henry on the head and then disappears into the crowd.

"Mrs. Charles!" you shout. But you can't be heard over the noise as people scramble to get into lifeboats. As the boat is lowered, you look up. The electric lights of the ship are still shining brightly.

Once the lifeboat is in the water, several men begin rowing away from the ship. From here you can see how much of the ship's bow is underwater. "It won't be long now," you think, as you clutch Henry tightly.

Turn the page.

"Hello there," a familiar voice says softly. You turn and see Emilie and Mrs. Robert in the lifeboat with you. "Looks like we survived," is all you manage to say.

"We're the lucky ones," Emilie says sadly. You bury your head in the baby's blanket and pray the rest of the family is as lucky as you two are.

THE END

To follow another path, turn to page 13.
To read the conclusion, turn to page 103.

Quickly Mr. Charles writes something on a piece of paper and hands it to you, along with a roll of cash.

"This is the address of our relatives in America," he whispers. "Make sure the children get to them."

Some families were separated as people escaped the sinking ship.

Turn the page.

You nod. Mr. Charles hands Agnes to the officer in charge of the lifeboat. You clutch Henry as the officer helps you, then James, into the lifeboat.

Mr. Charles tries to persuade Mrs. Charles to join you. She refuses, sobbing. As the boat is lowered, James and Agnes wave tearfully at their parents. Mr. Charles waves back. Mrs. Charles buries her head in her husband's coat.

An hour later it's all over. *Titanic* is gone. All you can think of is that you and the children have survived. You'll do your best to get them to their relatives in the United States.

THE END

To follow another path, turn to page 13.
To read the conclusion, turn to page 103.

You don't think it's a good idea to go back inside, but you must obey your employer. As you pass the grand staircase, you see Thomas Andrews. He helped design and build *Titanic*. He's urging everyone to put on life vests. The deck is tilting now. It's difficult to walk without stumbling.

The closer you get to the first-class area, the more a sense of doom fills you. "Please, we must go back to the lifeboats," you beg Mrs. Charles. But she won't listen. "My place is with my husband, and my children's place is with me," she says. The sound of rushing water is coming from somewhere below, but she doesn't seem to notice it.

Turn the page.

You know you won't survive if you follow Mrs. Charles. Without a word you turn and run back to the deck. By the time you get there, all the wooden lifeboats are gone.

"I'm not going to panic," you think.

Several men have locked arms and made a ring around one of the collapsible boats. They are making sure only women and children get in. You run to the boat and pass through the ring of men. Soon after you get in, the boat is lowered into the water.

Everyone in the boat is silent as you watch the horror unfold. By now *Titanic* is sinking rapidly. People are jumping and falling into the water. The ship's stern lifts out of the water, higher and higher. Then it plunges into the sea and is gone.

About 3:30 a.m. the ship *Carpathia* sails into view. Rescue! You hope the Charles family somehow managed to survive as well.

THE END

To follow another path, turn to page 13.
To read the conclusion, turn to page 103.

Many passengers went on the boat deck to get fresh air.

CHAPTER 4

Be Prepared and Survive

On April 10, 1912, you and your father boarded *Titanic* in Southampton, England. You are headed to New York City. Father has a new job there, and you will get to meet your uncle for the first time. This trip is the first time you've felt happy since your mother's death a year ago.

Father has been busy, so you've spent your time discovering every part of the ship. You've met two other boys near your age and have become good friends. All of you are Boy Scouts, which is a new organization in England and the United States. You also like to get into mischief.

Today, Sunday, April 14, is no exception. Earlier you tried to sneak into the first-class dining saloon with your friend William Carter, who is traveling first class. But a steward realized you and your other friend, Billy Goodwin, are third-class passengers. He quickly shooed you out.

It's after 11 p.m. now. You're with Father, who is playing cards in the third-class smoking room, and you're bored. You're about to go to your cabin when William and Billy appear.

"I got away when everyone went to sleep," Billy says. "That's not easy when you've got a mother, father, and five brothers and sisters!"

"Mother and my sister Lucile went to bed hours ago. Father is probably in the first-class smoking lounge," William says to you. "Can you get away?"

Nodding, you follow your friends into the passageway outside. "Where shall we go?" Billy asks.

"We could sneak down into the boiler rooms," you suggest.

"I want to see my dog," William says. "We can go to the kennels up on deck."

To go to the boiler rooms, turn to page **80**.

To go to the kennels, turn to page **88**.

The three of you race downstairs until you get to the boiler rooms. *Titanic* has 29 massive boilers that provide power to the ship. Passengers aren't supposed to be in this area. But sometimes you've been able to sneak in before the firemen, who work the boilers, make you leave. You make your way to boiler room 6, which is near the bow of the ship.

Suddenly a metallic tearing sound fills the air. Water starts pouring into the room. An alarm sounds, and a red warning light above the watertight door flashes. Firemen are scrambling around, trying to figure out what's happening.

"Come on boys, follow me!" a fireman shouts. He picks you up one by one and hauls you up a ladder. The fireman barely has time to scramble up the ladder before the boiler room is flooded.

You, your friends, and several firemen lay on the floor of E deck, gasping for breath. "What happened?" you ask.

"Must've hit an iceberg," one of the firemen replies. "Don't worry, though. *Titanic* has 16 watertight compartments. As long as they're closed, the ship will stay afloat. You'd best be getting back to your families."

"A good Boy Scout is observant," you explain. "It's our job to observe what's happening before we report."

The fireman smiles. "You do that, son," he says. "But do it somewhere else. This is no place for children."

To go to the main deck, turn to page 82.

To go to your father, turn to page 83.

"Let's go ask Captain Smith what's going on," William says. The three of you go up to the bridge. The ship's commanders are stationed at this area of the ship's bow above the A deck. You know you're not supposed to be in this area, but this could be an emergency.

As you near the bridge, you see Captain Smith with Thomas Andrews, who helped design and build the ship. "We struck an iceberg, and the forepeak and both forward holds are flooded," Andrews says. "The mail room is flooded. Boiler Room 6 is flooded to a depth of 14 feet. Water is coming into Boiler Room 5."

You, Billy, and William look solemnly at each other. You shake hands, knowing you may never see one another again. Then you all rush to break the news to your families.

Father is still playing cards when you run in, breathless. "We've hit an iceberg!" you cry.

Everyone in the room stares at you.

"Nonsense," says an elderly man, turning back to his book.

"I did feel some kind of bump a few minutes ago," another man comments.

"The engines have stopped," Father says, putting down his cards. "Tell me what's going on."

Quickly you tell him what happened.

"All right, son. I believe you," Father says, standing up. "But I'm not sure that it's serious. *Titanic* is practically unsinkable, after all." Father waves to a steward rushing past the lounge and asks him what's going on.

"Put your life vests on immediately, and go to the boat deck," he says impatiently.

Turn the page.

Surprised, Father says, "Do we have time to go back to our cabins?"

"You don't have time for anything," the steward says before rushing off.

"I don't believe him," Father says. "I'm going back for our things. You can come along or meet me on the boat deck."

Many crew members gave their lives to save the ship's passengers.

To go with your father, go to page 85.

To go to the deck, turn to page 87.

The hallway seems to be tilting, and it's hard to walk. In the cabin you put on several layers of woolen clothing and your overcoat.

"Boy Scouts are always prepared!" you exclaim as you grab your pocketknife. Father takes some personal items, money, and a photo of your mother.

Two stewards are banging on doors. They yell for people to put on their life vests. Most people have thrown overcoats over their pajamas. Some return to their cabins and lock the doors.

Third class is a confusing maze of hallways. But you've spent the last four days exploring, so you know every one by heart. "This way to the stairs, Father," you say, leading him down the hall. When you get to the staircase, there's water trickling down it.

*To go up the stairs, turn to page **86**.*

*To go down the hallway, turn to page **93**.*

"This is the shortest way to the deck," you say, ignoring the water on the stairs. "There's no straight way to get to the upper decks from third class. We'll have to go over C deck, then past the second-class library and the first-class dining saloon. Then we'll take the grand staircase to the boat deck."

Father is impressed. "I see you take the Boy Scout rule 'be observant' seriously," he says. "It might just save us."

As you pass the first-class dining saloon, you spot Billy with his family. They look panicked. "Have you seen my little sister Jessie?" Billy asks anxiously. "We were separated. Mother is frantic!"

"We'll help you look," you say.

"No, I'll help them," Father says. "You go to the boat deck and wait. I'll only be a few minutes."

The boat deck is crowded with people. J. Bruce Ismay, the chairman of the White Star Line, is urging passengers to put on their life vests.

"Get into a lifeboat, son," Ismay tells you.

"I can't," you reply. "I'm waiting for my father."

"Then put on this life vest," he says, strapping a life vest over your coat. He then heads toward the bridge. Just then Father appears at your side. "Good boy," he says. "A Boy Scout is obedient, and I see you are too."

The two of you approach a lifeboat. "Women and children only!" the officer shouts.

"I'm with my son," Father calls, pointing to you.

"Sorry, sir, only women and children," he says. "Your son can come aboard."

To get on this lifeboat, turn to page **94**.

To look for another lifeboat, turn to page **95**.

William's dog wags his tail as the three of you pet him. William makes sure the kennel is clean and has plenty of water.

"So what now?" you ask as you leave the kennels. Billy looks out over the deck and gasps, "Look at that!"

Directly in front of the ship is an enormous iceberg. *Titanic* is heading straight for it!

The ship starts to turn away from the iceberg, but bumps against it. A shudder goes though the ship. Huge chunks of ice break off the iceberg and fall onto the lower deck.

"Let's go play in the ice!" William shouts. You all run down to the deck and start throwing big chunks of ice around.

"Hey, the ship has stopped," Billy says. He's right. The engines are quiet.

Just then William's parents and sister appear on deck.

"Boys, come with us," his father says sternly. "They're loading some lifeboats from the promenade deck."

"No, sir," Billy says, "I need to find my family." Billy runs back toward third class.

You follow William's family to the promenade deck, which is enclosed with glass windows. An officer there says, "The captain thinks it will be easier to load some of the boats from here, so you can stay warm. Wait here for further orders."

There's some trouble opening the windows. Everyone is ordered to the boat deck. Then you're ordered back to the promenade deck, then back and forth again! No one seems to know what to do.

Turn the page.

The sky lights up with a white rocket. "That's a distress signal," Mr. Carter says.

"I must find my father!" you say. Mr. Carter grabs you by the shoulders.

"The officers aren't letting men on the boats, but they are loading women and children. If you go look for your father, you will likely not survive."

To Look for Father, go to page **91**.

To stay with the Carters, turn to page **97**.

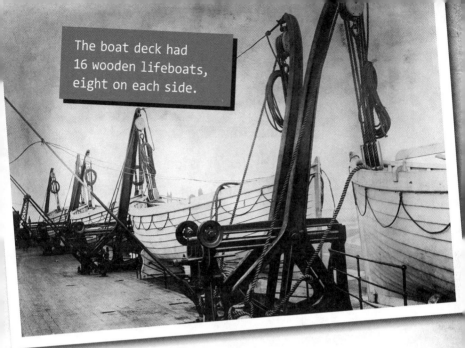

The boat deck had 16 wooden lifeboats, eight on each side.

"Still, I must try," you insist. Mr. Carter nods and lets you go. You run toward third class as fast as you can, but much of it is underwater now. You're not sure what to do.

"Be prepared," you think, fingering the pocketknife in your coat. "Father would look for me on the boat deck, not on the promenade deck!" You run back upstairs, but it's too late. All the lifeboats are gone. A familiar shape stands beside the railing.

Turn the page.

"Father!" you shout. He turns around and lifts you into his arms.

"We don't have much time," he says. "Our best bet is to stay out of the water for as long as we can. But we don't want to get sucked under with the ship. We can either jump now or wait until the boat goes under."

To jump now, turn to page **99.**

To wait, turn to page **101.**

Father follows you down the hall, which is starting to fill with water. At the top of the stairs is a locked door. Several other third-class passengers are there too. Everyone yells for someone to come, but no one does. The water is coming in faster now.

"I don't think we're going to make it, son," Father says, taking you in his arms. "Don't be afraid. We're together."

You close your eyes and hug Father tight. That's where you are when the water rushes through third class, drowning everyone.

THE END

To follow another path, turn to page 13.
To read the conclusion, turn to page 103.

"I won't leave without you," you say. Father shakes his head. "I'll get on the next boat, son. I'll see you in New York!"

Father hugs you tightly. Reluctantly you climb into the lifeboat with about 20 other people, all women and children. As the boat is lowered, you wave at your father and try not to cry. He smiles and waves back.

The next morning when the ship *Carpathia* rescues you and the other survivors, you search for your father. But you know in your heart you won't find him. You'll be traveling to New York alone.

THE END

To follow another path, turn to page 13.
To read the conclusion, turn to page 103.

Several boats are being loaded, but none of them are filled. "Why aren't they filling the boats?" you ask Father.

"Maybe there are so many lifeboats that they don't need to fill these," Father replies.

"Actually, there are only 20 lifeboats," you reply. "That means that there aren't enough boats for everyone on the ship."

One of the officers spies you and Father. "You there," he calls. "Do you have any experience with boats?"

"Yes," Father responds, surprised. "I sailed in my youth."

"Get on this boat," the officer says. "We need experienced sailors to guide the lifeboats."

Turn the page.

You and Father jump into the boat. After several more passengers are loaded, the officer gives the order to lower the boat. Once you're on the water, Father takes charge. He shows the others how to row the lifeboat.

There's nothing to do now but watch the great ship sink. It's a horrible sight as hundreds of people are thrown into the freezing water. *Titanic* finally slides into the ocean and is gone for good. After about 30 minutes the screams grow quiet. Now there's nothing to do but try to stay warm and wait for rescue. At least you and Father have survived.

THE END

To follow another path, turn to page 13.
To read the conclusion, turn to page 103.

Finally the officers get the windows open and Boat 4 in position. They stack deck chairs next to the window so people can climb out into the lifeboat. Officer Charles Lightoller helps you, William, Lucile, and Mrs. Carter into the boat. They wave tearfully to Mr. Carter.

Lightoller orders the boat to be lowered. By now *Titanic* has sunk so far that the lifeboat only drops a few feet before it hits the water. Two crew members row as hard as they can to get away from the ship before it sinks.

You don't know how you make it through the terrible, cold night. You and William take turns pounding on each other's feet and legs to keep warm. About 3:30 a.m. a ship appears on the horizon. It's the *Carpathia*. You're hauled up to the ship with a rope. An officer takes your name. "Go into the dining saloon. There's hot soup for everyone there," he says kindly.

Turn the page.

You are stumbling toward the dining saloon when suddenly you're caught up in a bone-crushing hug. "Father," you gasp.

"When the ship went down, I climbed onto some wreckage. A lifeboat picked me up," Father explains.

Later you find out that Billy's family didn't survive the sinking. So many people died. You and Father are two of the lucky survivors.

THE END

To follow another path, turn to page 13.
To read the conclusion, turn to page 103.

"Let's go now," you say.

"All right. When I tell you to go, jump with me."

You stand at the railing with Father as the ship tilts farther upward. Soon you can't keep your footing. The seawater is rushing toward you when Father yells, "Take a deep breath, and jump as far as you can. I'll be right with you!"

The cold water tears through you with a pain you've never felt before. You barely hold your breath long enough to get to the surface.

The water is filled with wreckage. There's a tangle of ropes and heavy wooden doors in front of you. Your frozen fingers somehow open the pocketknife. You saw at the ropes until they loosen, and one of the doors breaks free. Painfully you climb onto it.

Turn the page.

"Father!" you shout until you become hoarse, but you can't see him. Some time later a lifeboat appears, and several strong hands haul you up. You feel frozen, but not just from the cold. You've survived, but Father is gone forever.

THE END

To follow another path, turn to page 13.
To read the conclusion, turn to page 103.

The stern rises higher in the air until the ship is straight up. Screaming passengers tumble past you. The ship balances for a moment. Then it begins to plunge into the water.

"Take my hand!" Father yells. Father jumps and pulls you with him. The water is unbelievably cold, but you manage to hold your breath. You're pulled under. You fight your way to the surface, still clasping Father's hand.

Together you start swimming, hanging onto floating wreckage. A lifeboat appears in the darkness. With all the strength you have left, you paddle toward it. Rough hands grab you and pull you up. Someone throws a blanket around you.

"You and your father are lucky to survive," a voice says. "You'll be fine now."

THE END

To follow another path, turn to page 13.
To read the conclusion, turn to page 103.

Titanic survivors gathered together after their rescue.

CHAPTER 5

Why Did Some Survive?

Of more than 2,200 people on *Titanic* on that terrible night, only 705 survived. Survival depended on many things. Most people survived by luck, but a few understood what was happening and made the right choices.

More third-class passengers—about 536—died than any other class. Several things worked against them. Many third-class cabins were in the bow of the ship. They were the first to flood when the ship hit the iceberg.

The third-class area was also separated from the rest of the ship. This was because of fears that third-class passengers would carry diseases. On *Titanic* many third-class passengers couldn't find their way out to the lifeboats. Also, some third-class passengers didn't speak English. They couldn't understand the crew members' instructions.

First- and second-class passengers were more likely to survive, but only women and children. The idea of "women and children first" was a strong one at the time of the disaster. Many survivors told stories of how men sacrificed themselves so that women and children could live.

Passengers who understood the danger early were more likely to live. When *Titanic*'s officers began loading the lifeboats, few passengers were willing to leave the warm ship. Most lifeboats were only partially filled when they launched. By the time the rest of the passengers realized the danger, it was too late.

Water rushed over the grand staircase as *Titanic* sank.

For male passengers, the side of the boat deck they went to made a difference. Second Officer Charles Lightoller supervised the lifeboat boarding on the port side of the deck. He allowed few men to board these boats. First Officer William Murdoch supervised the boarding of boats on the starboard side. He allowed more men to board.

More than 1,500 people went into the water when *Titanic* sank. As many as 1,000 were probably still alive. The key to survival was to quickly get out of the freezing ocean water. *Titanic*'s lifeboats did rescue a few people from the water. Most of these people lived.

The woolen clothing commonly worn at the time of the disaster also helped people survive, especially if they went into the water. Wet wool acts as an insulator. It keeps skin warmer than the synthetic fabrics people wear today.

The *Titanic* disaster shocked the world. The biggest reason so many died was the lack of lifeboats. Also, there were no standard rules for getting passengers off the ship during an emergency.

Today the world is still interested in *Titanic*. Movies, books, TV shows, and plays tell the story of that desperate night and the people who survived it—and those who didn't.

REAL SURVIVORS

William Carter—Eleven-year-old William Carter
was traveling first-class with his parents and older sister.
He, his mother, and sister all survived the sinking,
even though the crew member loading the lifeboat
at first refused to let him on. The crew member also
refused to let William bring his dog, which upset him
very much. Millionaire businessman John Jacob Astor
comforted William by telling him he would take care
of the dog. Both Astor and the dog died in the disaster.
Unfortunately, William's friend Billy Goodwin also died,
along with his entire family.

Emilie Kreuchen and Rosalie Bidois—Ladies'
maids Emilie Kreuchen and Rosalie Bidois boarded
lifeboats with their employers, Elisabeth Walton
Robert and Madeleine Astor. All four women survived
the disaster.

Margaret Brown—Margaret Brown was a wealthy
woman traveling with her friends, John Jacob and
Madeleine Astor. She is famous for helping load other
passengers into lifeboats and for encouraging the other
women in her boat to join her in rowing to safety. After
the disaster, she set up a fund for *Titanic* survivors and
worked to win women the right to vote. She died in 1932.

Millvina Dean—At 2 months, 27 days old, Millvina Dean was the youngest passenger on *Titanic*. She and her older brother were traveling third-class with their parents to the United States. Her father planned to open a store in Wichita, Kansas. Dean, her mother, and her brother survived, but her father died. The family returned to England, where Dean lived until she died May 31, 2009, at age 97. She was the last living survivor of the *Titanic* sinking.

Survival Quiz

1. When you learned that the ship struck the iceberg, what was the best thing to do?

A. Put on your life vest and warm clothes and go up to the deck.

B. Stay in your cabin and wait for further instructions.

C. Make sure all of your possessions are safe.

2. What was the smartest thing to do when boarding a lifeboat?

A. Wait on deck to see if the situation is really serious before boarding a boat.

B. Try to find your family or friends to make sure that you get on the same lifeboat.

C. Get on a lifeboat right away, and row away from the ship.

3. If you ended up in the water, what was the best thing to do?

A. Tread water.

B. Swim to a lifeboat as quickly as possible.

C. Grab onto a piece of debris and float on it until the rescue ship comes.

Answers: A, C, B

Can You Survive
AN
EARTHQUAKE?

An Interactive Survival Adventure

by Rachael Hanel

Consultant:
April Kelcy
Emergency Management Consultant
Earthquake Solutions

TABLE OF CONTENTS

About Your Adventure 115

Chapter 1
An Unpredictable Moment 117

Chapter 2
Disaster in Alaska 125

Chapter 3
Earthquake in the City 155

Chapter 4
A Quake and a Big Wave 185

Chapter 5
Surviving an Earthquake 211

Real Survivors 216
Survival Quiz 218

About Your
ADVENTURE

YOU are about to experience one of the most unpredictable events in nature—an earthquake! You have no warning. How will you stay alive?

In this book you'll deal with extreme survival situations. You'll explore how the knowledge you have and the choices you make can mean the difference between life and death.

Chapter One sets the scene. Then you choose which path to read. Follow the directions at the bottom of each page. The choices you make will change your outcome. After you finish one path, go back and read the others for new perspectives and more adventures.

YOU CHOOSE the path
you take through your adventure.

Earthquakes strike without warning and can cause enormous damage.

CHAPTER 1

An Unpredictable Moment

Imagine a bright, sunny day. People are outside walking, running, or relaxing. Then without warning, the ground starts to shake. Trees topple and buildings crumble. People panic and scream. The shaking lasts only moments, but the entire landscape changes.

Earthquakes strike with little warning. Unlike other natural disasters such as hurricanes and tornadoes, there's nothing to see before they occur.

Earthquakes strike when tectonic plates below Earth's surface shift and move. Most earthquakes occur at fault lines—the places where the tectonic plates intersect.

Turn the page.

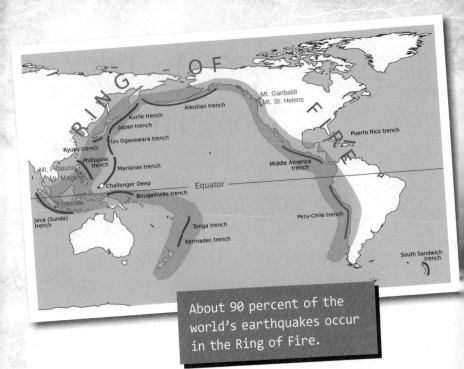

R I N G   O F   F I R E

Mt. Garibaldi
Mt. St. Helens
Aleutian trench
Kurile trench
Japan trench
Izu Ogasawara trench
Ryuku trench
Philippine trench
Marianas trench
Mt. Pinatubo
Mt. Mayon
Challenger Deep
Bougainville trench
Equator
Puerto Rico trench
Middle America trench
Krakatau
Java (Sunda) trench
Tonga trench
Kermadec trench
Peru-Chile trench
South Sandwich trench

About 90 percent of the world's earthquakes occur in the Ring of Fire.

Earthquakes are more likely to happen in the Ring of Fire. This area is around the edges of the Pacific Ocean. It includes Japan, Indonesia, and the coasts of Alaska, Chile, and California.

But even locations far away from the ocean can experience big earthquakes. The New Madrid fault system runs 150 miles from Illinois to Tennessee, also affecting parts of Indiana, Missouri, Arkansas, Kentucky, and Mississippi. South Carolina also has a major fault line. Around the world, earthquakes strike along fault lines in the Arabian Peninsula, east Africa, and the Mediterranean Sea.

Earthquakes are measured on the Richter scale. The strongest earthquakes have measured more than 9.0. These include measurements of 9.5 in Chile in 1960, 9.2 in Alaska in 1964, and 9.1 off the coast of Sumatra in 2004.

Because earthquakes can strike without warning, it is important to have a disaster plan in place. The U.S. Geological Survey distributes information about what to do before, during, and after an earthquake.

Turn the page.

If you live in an earthquake region, make sure your home is safe. Falling household objects often injure people. Make sure pictures and mirrors are securely fastened to walls. Secure top-heavy furniture to wall studs with the use of brackets. Tie down TVs and computer monitors with nylon straps or buckles that can be easily removed and relocated.

Create an emergency plan. Will you know where to reunite with family and friends in case you get separated? Keep a flashlight and shoes near your bed, in case an earthquake occurs during the night. The flashlight should be approved by the Mine Safety and Health Administration. These flashlights have been tested in dangerous conditions and will not give off sparks that could trigger gas explosions. Families in earthquake areas should have disaster kits. These kits include medicine, bottled water, snacks, batteries, a battery-operated radio, and heavy-duty plastic bags.

The USGS also offers suggestions for how to protect yourself when an earthquake starts. If you are indoors, drop, cover, and hold on. Get under a sturdy piece of furniture. If you can't do that, stay by an interior wall and protect your head and neck with your arms. Don't go outside until you are sure the earthquake is over.

If you are caught outside, get to an open area. Avoid sidewalks or areas near tall buildings. If you are in a car, pull over to the side of the road as soon as possible and stay in the car. Avoid bridges and overpasses, because they might collapse.

Turn the page.

If you're near the ocean, try to find higher ground after the initial shaking stops. Earthquakes can trigger huge waves called tsunamis.

Once it is safe to get up, move carefully so that you don't trip over fallen objects or run into debris hanging from the ceiling. It's usually best to leave the building until you know that it's safe. Damaged buildings are at risk for collapse, fires, or natural gas explosions.

You should know where shelters might be located. They usually are set up in buildings that can hold many people, such as school gymnasiums or community centers. Keep in mind that it may take some time for emergency officials to find the safest building for a shelter.

After an earthquake, emergency workers may be too overwhelmed to help everyone. In many communities, people can take Community Emergency Response Team (CERT) classes. With proper training, ordinary citizens can help themselves and others.

*To experience an earthquake in rural Alaska, turn to page **125**.*

*To experience an earthquake in a city, turn to page **155**.*

*For an island earthquake, turn to page **185**.*

Spring comes late in northern Alaska.

CHAPTER 2

Disaster in Alaska

The snow has been lightly falling all day. It's late March, but spring won't arrive for at least two months here in Alaska. You live in the remote woods several hours north of Anchorage. This time of year, the sun comes up late and goes down early. The chill lingers in the air for months.

You haven't had a lot of work lately. The construction business slows down in the winter. It will get busier in the summer. You pick up side jobs here and there when you can.

Just as you sit down to eat lunch, your phone rings. It's your friend Jeff.

Turn the page.

Fishing is a major industry in Alaska.

"I just heard about some work on the docks in Valdez," he says. "Do you want to go?"

Valdez is a few hours away. You prefer to work closer to home. You look at your dog, Buddy. You hate leaving him behind for that long. But you know dock work pays well, even though the work is hard.

"Let me think about it."

"OK," Jeff says. "Call me back soon. I plan to leave in a few hours."

*To go to Valdez, turn to page **128**.*

*To stay home, turn to page **129**.*

You pick up the phone to call Jeff. "OK, let's go. My neighbor said he'd watch my dog."

On the drive, you look out the window at the majestic mountains and thick stands of trees. Alaska is a beautiful but wild place. There's a lot of wide-open spaces between the towns.

You arrive in Valdez late in the afternoon. "What should we do?" Jeff asks. "We could go down to the docks now and see if we can get some work, or we could get a motel room and start fresh in the morning."

If you wait until morning, there might not be any work left. You know of many people who have come here looking for work in the last few days. But you're awfully tired. A good night of rest will help you feel better.

To go to the docks right away, turn to page 132.

To check in at a motel, turn to page 136.

You call Jeff. "I'm going to stay home," you tell him. A few hours later, you're cooking dinner. You're in your kitchen near the stove when you hear a low rumbling. You grab the counter as your cupboard doors fly open. Dishes and cans of food hit the floor. Beneath your feet, the ground is shaking violently. It's an earthquake!

Outside, trees are bending low to the ground and snapping, as if hit by strong winds. A large crack opens in the ground. The bricks in your chimney collapse. After several seconds, the quaking stops.

Earthquakes can create huge cracks in roads.

Turn the page.

The house is dark. You grab a flashlight from a drawer. You have made sure to buy only Mine Safety and Health Administration-approved flashlights. You know they will work and will be safe in an emergency.

You look at the damage in your house. Several cracks have appeared in your walls. The kitchen is a mess, with broken dishes and food all over the floor. Your electricity is off. The gas for your stove and furnace is not working. Your house phone and cell phone are both dead.

What should you do now? You don't have any heat or electricity. You wonder about the gas lines. They may have been badly damaged, which could create a dangerous situation. The air in the house will soon turn cold, and you're not sure when help will arrive in this remote area.

You think about your neighbors Jane and Tom. They are in their 70s and have some health problems. Maybe you should try to check on them. But the roads likely are badly damaged.

To stay in your house, turn to page 139.

To drive to the neighbors' house, turn to page 145.

You head down to the docks, located on the edge of town on Prince William Sound. Valdez is a main fishing and shipping port in Alaska. Many goods first come into Valdez by ship and are taken into Alaska's interior by train or truck. There might be some work unloading freight and fish from the ships and boats.

You spy a man with a clipboard at one of the docks.

"Excuse me," you say. "Do you know of any work around here? We work in construction, but we're laid off right now. We were hoping to get some work for a few days."

The man looks both of you up and down. "All right, you're in luck," he says gruffly. "Some of my guys didn't show up today. We got a boat full of fish arriving in about a half-hour. Can you stick around?"

"Sure!" you say. "Thanks a lot."

The boat comes in. You stand on the end of the dock with a few other guys. Suddenly, the dock shifts below your feet and you hear a low rumbling sound. You look around. The dock is rippling up and down. You lose your balance and fall down.

"What's going on?" Jeff yells.

You look toward town, and you watch buildings buckle and collapse. Trees are swaying and bouncing.

"It's an earthquake!" you scream as the dock below you collapses, spilling you and the rest of the men into the water. You inhale sharply as the icy water hits your skin. The fishing boat slams into part of the dock. You hear men scream in pain.

Turn the page.

"Jeff! Jeff!" you yell frantically, treading water as you scan the area. But there's no sight of him. Your arms and legs feel like blocks of ice. If you don't get to the shore now, you will be too cold to make it. You use all your strength to swim to the shore and pull yourself out of the water. Other men gather ropes and life preservers to rescue the ones who were sucked into the bay. You can't see Jeff, though. Where could he be?

Police officers and firefighters arrive after a few minutes. They gather rescue equipment and prepare to go into the water. An officer checks on you.

"We need you to evacuate," she says. "The town isn't safe. We're at risk for aftershocks, and it's likely that we'll get a tsunami within a few minutes. This is a very dangerous situation."

"But my friend is in the water!" you say. "I want to stay here until he's found!"

"We have a rescue team going in," she says. "We'll find your friend. You need to leave now."

You know you can help find Jeff. You could tell rescuers exactly where he went in. But the police officer is right. Maybe you should leave the rescue effort to the professionals.

To follow the officer's advice to evacuate, turn to page 142.

To stay, turn to page 147.

"Let's get some rest tonight and start fresh tomorrow," you say.

"Sounds good to me," Jeff says.

You drive to a motel. You check into the room and start unpacking when the floor starts to shake violently beneath your feet. Jeff says, "What's going on?"

A lamp on the table falls to the floor, and cracks appear in the walls. A loud rumbling sound fills your ears. The ground continues to shift beneath you.

"It's an earthquake!" you yell. "It feels like the building is going to collapse! Let's get out of here!"

You and Jeff run outside. Trees sway back and forth. One falls on Jeff's truck, crushing it. Windows break and shards of glass fall to the ground. The force of the quake knocks you to your knees. You both curl up, trying to protect your bodies from falling debris.

After a few seconds, the shaking stops. Everything is quiet. Then sirens start to sound. Rescue efforts are underway. A police car travels down the street and stops in front of you. When the officer hears that you ran out of the motel during the quake, he scolds you. "Don't you know that is one of the most dangerous things you can do?"

"I guess we panicked," Jeff replies. "Do you know where a shelter is located?"

"Head to the elementary school," the officer says. "We hear that building was not damaged. Volunteers will set up shelter there."

At the school, you sit down next to a group of people and overhear them talking about leaving town. They are heading toward Anchorage, a couple of hours away.

Turn the page.

"Do you have room in your vehicle for two more?" you ask the driver, Joe.

"Sure, you're welcome to come with us," Joe says. "We just haven't decided which way to go. The roads likely are damaged. They might soon be closing the main highways. It might be best to take the smaller, inland roads. The police don't have the resources to block off every road. What do you guys think?"

To take the inland route, turn to page 149.

To take the highway to Anchorage, turn to page 150.

It's best to stay where you are. You saw the large cracks in the earth around your house. This is a rugged area. The roads are surrounded by rocky hillsides. An aftershock could easily trigger a landslide.

You shut off the gas lines to the house. The propane tank outside, which supplies gas to your stove and furnace, may have been damaged. The gas lines underneath the ground could be broken. Gas leaks could cause an explosion.

Without heat, it will get cold soon. You gather thick clothing and blankets. After a few hours, despite the thick layers, you still are very cold. Now it's dark, and you're sure you don't want to venture out into the unknown. But when will help arrive?

Turn the page.

You shiver uncontrollably. You decide to start a fire in the fireplace, forgetting that your chimney is damaged. You don't realize that you are in the first stages of hypothermia. The cold is affecting your ability to make good decisions.

You gather newspapers and firewood you have stacked in your entryway. You light a match and are pleased at the warmth that comes from the fireplace. Soon you have a roaring fire going. But after a few minutes, smoke starts to fill the house. You cough and your eyes water. You feel your way to the doorway and stumble out the front door. Buddy, your dog, follows you. Outside, you take deep breaths of the cold air.

After a few moments, a truck rumbles into your yard. It's Jack, your nearest neighbor, who lives a few miles away.

"Are you OK?" Jack asks. "I thought I'd check on the neighbors. Who knows when emergency crews will arrive?"

"Yes, I'm OK, except I built a fire and now the house is full of smoke. I'm going to collect some snow to put out the fire."

"Forget about the house," Jack says. "Come with me where it's safe."

"I'm not sure it's any safer on the roads," you say. "An aftershock could occur at any moment. Besides, the fire is pretty small. It won't take much to put it out."

To go with Jack, turn to page 151.

To put out the fire, turn to page 152.

The police officer helps you get up. "You need to get moving," she says. "Head toward downtown. You'll find relief workers who can get you into some dry clothes."

You take a moment to glance back at the water. Rescue boats are already in the bay, looking for survivors. The officer pushes you forward. "Let's go," she says. You think about sprinting toward the water, but you're too tired. She tells you to go to the elementary school downtown, where a shelter has been set up. You shiver as you walk slowly toward the school.

In the school gymnasium, volunteers are setting up cots and tables. Much to your relief, you see Jeff!

"Rescue workers pulled me out of the water right away," he says. "I was so scared."

You give him a hug. "I'm so glad you're all right. Let's sit down and warm up."

A group of people is talking next to you.

"We're going to head out of town," a man named Joe says. "We don't feel safe here. We're going to head back toward Anchorage."

"Do you have room in your car for two more?" you ask Joe. "We live near Anchorage, and our truck is back at the dock."

"Sure," Joe says. "Let's go."

Anchorage, Alaska, was the site of a 9.2-magnitude earthquake in March 1964.

Turn the page.

A few of you pile into a van. "Which way should we go?" asks Joan, Joe's wife. "I heard the relief workers say that many of the main highways and bridges are damaged."

"Well, we could take the main highway and see how far we get," you say. "But it might be faster to take some of the smaller roads inland. It's a little out of our way, but maybe they weren't as badly damaged as the roads near the coast."

As a group, you have to decide. What would be the best way to leave Valdez?

To take the inland route, turn to page **149**.

To take the highway, turn to page **150**.

You load Buddy into your truck and head to Jane and Tom's. You want to make sure they're OK. You're glad to see the road is in fairly good shape. You have to dodge a few cracks in the road and some boulders, but you're able to pass through.

Jane and Tom are safe in their house.

"We're going to wait here for a few hours in case there are more aftershocks," Tom says. "Then we're going to drive to Anchorage and find a shelter."

A 1994 earthquake destroyed an overpass in California.

Turn the page.

"That's a good idea," you say. "It's too cold to stay here for long. We don't want to build a fire in case a natural gas line has been broken." You all gather blankets and huddle together to keep warm through the night. At the first daylight, you drive toward Anchorage.

Your survival instincts have paid off. You stayed safe and lived through a major earthquake.

THE END

To follow another path, turn to page 123.
To read the conclusion, turn to page 211.

You find rescue workers launching boats into the water.

"Over there!" You point to where you last saw Jeff. "My friend went into the water right over there. Please try to find him!"

You watch the boat zigzag slowly through the water. The rescue workers come up with nothing. You're starting to feel desperate. Will they ever find Jeff? Is he even still alive?

You hear a crackle from a rescue worker's two-way radio. "Everybody leave the area!" the voice says. "A tsunami is heading this way!"

"Get back to shore!" the worker screams into the radio at the boats in the water. The boats start to quickly come to shore. Still no sight of Jeff. The worker looks at you. "Get out of here! It's not safe!" he yells.

Turn the page.

You turn around and see a huge wave about 40 feet high. It's headed straight for you! You try to run, but it's too late. The wall of water slams the shore and sweeps you away, along with everyone else on the shore and in the harbor. You all become victims of the deadly tsunami.

THE END

To follow another path, turn to page 123.
To read the conclusion, turn to page 211.

The group decides to take the less traveled roads. You plan to head north for a while, then turn to go west toward Anchorage. You are surprised that the roads are in fairly good shape. Going the inland route was the right choice.

After several hours you arrive in Anchorage. Police officers on the edge of town direct you to a shelter. There you find warm food and a cot. You stand in line to use a phone to call your family. In the next day or so, law enforcement officers will escort you to your home to check on the damage. You have safely made it through the earthquake and its aftermath.

THE END

To follow another path, turn to page 123.
To read the conclusion, turn to page 211.

Your group decides to take the highway. A line of vehicles heads out of Valdez. The roads are damaged but passable. The earthquake's force amazes you. Parts of the road have shifted entirely. Outside of the van's window, you noticed that train cars in the rail yard have flipped on their sides.

At one of the bridges, traffic slows. Some drivers are turning their cars around because they think the bridge is unsafe. Joe keeps going forward. When you're on the bridge, you hear a low rumble. "What's that noise?" one of the women asks. It takes you a second to realize what's happening.

"It's an aftershock!" you yell.

The quaking has caused a large crack in the bridge. Seconds later, the van plunges into the water. You are one of many casualties in this Alaska earthquake.

THE END

To follow another path, turn to page 123.
To read the conclusion, turn to page 211.

"I really think you should come with me," Jack says. "The house just isn't safe."

You look at your dog and then look at the house. You worry that the fire could get of control, but you know you can't go back in there. "You're right, Jack. Let's go."

The roads here are remote, but overall there isn't as much damage as you feared. A few miles down the road, you reach the house of your neighbors Tom and Jane. To your relief, they are not hurt.

"Jump in," Jack tells them. "Let's go to Anchorage. We can take a more inland route. Roads should be less damaged there. We can find a shelter and let our families know we're OK."

You are still worried about your house, but at least you and Buddy are safe.

THE END

To follow another path, turn to page 123.
To read the conclusion, turn to page 211.

"Jack, the fire is really small. Just help me get some snow, and I know I can put it out."

Jack agrees to help you. Both of you collect snow in 5-gallon buckets you have in your garage. When the buckets are filled, you go into the house.

"I'm going to stay out here," Jack says. Buddy stays behind too.

When you get into the house, there's much more smoke than before. You go to the fireplace and dump the snow on the fire, but to your dismay, you see that it has spread to nearby furniture. There's now a full-fledged blaze in your house.

You start to gasp from the thick smoke. You can't see in front of you. Blindly, you try to feel your way out of the house, but you collapse a few feet from the front door.

You can hear Jack yelling your name outside the door, but you know it's too late for him to save you. A damaged house after an earthquake is a dangerous place to be. Staying here has cost you your life.

THE END

To follow another path, turn to page 123.
To read the conclusion, turn to page 211.

The Bay Bridge connects San Francisco to Oakland, California.

CHAPTER 3

Earthquake in the City

Your workday is almost over. You pack your laptop in your bag and leave the newspaper office in San Francisco. As you head out the door, your cell phone rings. It's your best friend, Ann. "I'm having a few people over for dinner tonight," she says. "Why don't you join us?"

You pause for a moment before answering. You've been on the go all day. You would love to hang out with friends, but you would like to go home and change into comfortable clothes first.

"What time?"

"Come over right away," Ann says. "I know you too well. If you go home first, you probably will stay there all night!"

155

Turn the page.

She's right. Ann lives in the market district of the city. You live in Oakland, several miles away across the bay.

"Let me call you back in a few minutes," you tell her.

To go home, go to page **157**.

To go to your friend's house, turn to page **161**.

You call Ann back. "I'm just going to head home. It's been a long day. Let's get together this weekend."

In your car, you notice how the reddish-orange light from the sunset reflects in the water of the bay as you drive across the bridge. It's a beautiful day. Not a cloud in the sky, and hardly any wind.

After you cross the bridge, you're on the interstate highway when you see the strangest thing. The road before you is rippling up and down, like an ocean wave. Cars ahead of you hurtle into the air and come crashing back down onto the pavement. It's an earthquake! The screeching sound of metal on pavement fills your ears. You hit the brakes hard when you feel the road below you give way.

You're on the top level of a two-level interstate. Before you know it, the top level crashes down onto the lower level. You scream in horror as you fall.

Turn the page.

The Cypress Freeway in Oakland collapsed during a 1989 earthquake.

Your stomach feels like it's on a roller coaster. Your car hits the pavement with a loud thump. You're stunned, but nothing seems to be broken or badly injured. You have survived an earthquake—so far. But aftershocks could arrive at any moment.

You feel trapped and start to panic. All you can think about is getting out of this small space. You try to open your car door, but it's stuck. You bang your shoulder against the door a couple of times, and it flies open. You tumble out of the car.

"Are you OK?" says a man who comes running up to your side.

"I … I … I think so," you stammer as you get to your feet.

Screams fill the air. You have escaped serious injury, but several others have not. You look around at the destruction. Cars are crumpled like balls of paper. Large sections of roadway have collapsed.

"My name is Ray, and I'm a firefighter," says the man who helped you. "Why don't you head to the high school a few blocks west? That school is a shelter in the city's emergency plan. If the school has been damaged, someone there will tell you where to go. But be careful. The earthquake has probably damaged power lines."

"OK," you say, still dazed and in shock. Then a piercing scream gets your full attention. It's coming from below. "Help me! Help me!" a woman shouts.

Ray sprints to a spot in the road that has cracked open. He can see below to the lower level of the interstate. Other people run to his side.

"We have to get down there!" he shouts.

You could stay and help. You are small. Perhaps you could reach the woman more easily than the larger men who have gathered. But an aftershock could happen at any moment, further collapsing the road.

To stay and help rescue workers, turn to page 162.

To head to the shelter, turn to page 171.

You call Ann. "I'm coming over," you say. "I'll be there in about 20 minutes."

At Ann's house, you go into the kitchen and help her cut up fruit for dinner. Just then, the ground beneath you starts to shake. The cupboards fly open, and dishes crash to the floor. You grab the edge of the counter to stay upright.

"It's an earthquake!" Ann screams. "What should we do?"

You try to think. You can either stay inside or run outside.

To stay inside, turn to page 166.

To run outside, turn to page 169.

The woman continues to scream. "Help me! Help me! I'm hurt!"

The screams are impossible to ignore. You run over to where the rescue group has gathered.

"That is a small space," Ray says, looking down below. "I'm not sure I can get down there."

"Let me go," you say.

You squeeze down into the hole. The jagged concrete rips through your clothes. There's barely enough room for your body, but you manage to wiggle down to the woman in the car.

"I can't get my door open!" cries the woman, who says her name is Tina.

You tug and pull at her car door, and it finally pops open. "Can you walk?" you ask.

"I think so," Tina says. "My arm and shoulder are really hurting, but I think I can walk."

You help Tina out of the car. You both walk to the opening where rescue workers wait above. You see Ray's arm reach down. Tina grabs his arm with her good arm, and you push her up from below. After she is safely on top, Ray grabs you and brings you up as well.

"Thank you," he says. "It would have taken us a lot longer to get to her if you weren't here."

Just then, you hear a loud rumbling.

Turn the page.

The ground shakes and stirs. It's an aftershock! You all hang on to one another. The rumbling lasts for just a few seconds. But in that time, the road has collapsed even more. The opening that you just came through is now completely blocked.

Several injured people sit at the side of the road. They are hurt too badly to walk to the shelter. The rescue workers on the scene have to first try to reach people trapped in their vehicles. They are practicing triage, where they help the most seriously injured people first.

"We need to get these people to a hospital," Ray says, pointing to the people sitting on the side of the road.

A man who arrived from a nearby house to offer help says, "I have a van. I can drive people to the hospital."

The man goes to get his van and returns a few minutes later. Ray turns to you. "We can use your help here," he says. "Or you could drive people to the hospital. Your choice."

To drive the injured people to the hospital, turn to page **178**.

To stay and help rescue people, turn to page **179**.

"Let's stay here!" you shout over the noise. Outside you see trees swaying and toppling. Both indoors and outdoors seem dangerous right now.

You and Ann take cover under a sturdy table. The ground continues to tremble and shake. You hear a loud roaring noise, like the earth is opening up all around you. You've never experienced anything like this.

Crack! You look up just in time to see a large chunk of plaster from the ceiling come crashing down. You made a good decision—the table protects you.

When the shaking is over, you get up and look around at the mess of broken dishes and spilled food. You slowly get to your feet.

A Santa Monica apartment building was destroyed in a 1994 earthquake.

You and Ann head outside and look at the damage. Houses have slid off their foundations. Trees are snapped in half. After a few moments of silence, the sirens scream.

"What should we do now?" you ask. "I'm not sure the house is safe."

Turn the page.

"We could stay and wait for rescue workers to tell us what to do next," Ann says. "Or we could try to find a shelter."

To stay at the house and wait for help, turn to page **174.**

To head to a shelter, turn to page **175.**

"I think we should go outside," you say.

You and Ann run out of the house. Trees are swaying. It's like an invisible hand is twisting them. Branches start to fall. One of them hits you and cuts you on the arm. A few feet away, a large crack opens in the earth with a loud roar. You feel like you're going to be swallowed into the earth. The ground beneath you rolls like a wave.

After a few seconds, the shaking stops. All is quiet for a moment. Then dogs start to bark and you hear screams and cries in the distance.

"What now?" Ann asks. "We shouldn't go back into the house. The damage has probably made it unstable. We can wait here for help. Or we can start walking to see if we can find a shelter."

*To stay at the house, turn to page **170**.*

*To find an emergency shelter, turn to page **175**.*

169

"Maybe we should check on my neighbors," Ann says. "Marge and George live a couple of houses down. I want to make sure they're OK."

On the street, you have to walk around fallen tree branches and jump over cracks in the road. You reach the neighbors' house. Marge is outside crying.

"What's wrong?" Ann asks her. "Are you hurt?"

"I think my leg is broken," she says. "And George is inside. I think he may be trapped!"

Your first instinct is to go inside to find George. But you know the inside of a house is not a safe place to be after an earthquake. You could try to run and get help. Maybe there is an emergency crew nearby.

To go inside the house, turn to page 181.

To find an emergency crew, turn to page 182.

Other people with minor injuries stumble from their cars.

"A firefighter told me to head to the school," you tell them. "If the building is not damaged, aid workers there can help us. We can go as a group."

You take the arm of a woman. She says her name is Betty. She appears to be in her 70s and is having trouble walking. "I hurt my knee," Betty says. "I don't know how far I can go."

"Let's get off the interstate," you say. "I hear sirens below. Someone may be able to help us." You and Betty carefully pick your way through the crumbled concrete. The streets look like war zones you've seen on TV. Large cracks split the roads. Branches and limbs from toppled trees are strewn through the streets and yards. Every house is damaged. Chimneys have fallen, and houses are twisted off their foundations.

Turn the page.

You've walked several blocks when you trip over a piece of debris. You drop Betty's arm as you land flat on your face on the hard concrete. "Ouch!" you cry. You've badly hurt your leg, and blood streams from a cut above your ear. You try to stand, but you can't seem to move.

"Are you all right?" Betty says.

"I think I twisted my ankle. And my head hurts." You hold your hand on the cut, trying to stop the flow of blood.

Betty starts yelling for help. Three teenage boys run over. "Don't worry, lady. We'll get you to the shelter." Two of the boys, Luke and Tyler, form a human chair with their arms to carry you. The other one, Jake, takes Betty's arm.

With the boys' help, you reach the school a short time later. Aid workers there get you the medical help you need. You're lucky that the boys were there—otherwise, the story could have ended very differently.

THE END

To follow another path, turn to page 123.
To read the conclusion, turn to page 211.

"Let's stay here," you say. "It seems safer."

Ann looks out the window. "The streets look pretty damaged. I hope someone will come to check on us soon."

You go back inside. Ann gets some blankets. Without electricity, a chill creeps into the air.

It quickly becomes dark. "Let's light some candles," Ann says. She goes into the kitchen to get matches and comes back into the living room. She gathers some candles on a coffee table and strikes a match.

BOOM! The flash of bright light and cracking sound jolt you. You and Ann are blown backward as the room fills with flames. In the earthquake, natural gas pipelines were cracked. Some of the invisible gas had filled the house. The match ignited the gas, and the resulting explosion cost both you and Ann your lives.

THE END

To follow another path, turn to page 123.
To read the conclusion, turn to page 211.

"Let's go to a shelter," you say. "We can try to get in touch with our families. I'm really worried about my mom and dad."

"But it's getting dark," Ann says. "I don't think it's a good idea to walk through the damage when we can't see."

"That's a good point," you say. "But we shouldn't go back into the house."

Turn the page.

"That's true. Let's put up a tent and camp out here tonight. We can try to find a shelter in the morning."

Ann has a tent and sleeping bags in her garage. You feel a lot safer staying in an open area. A couple of small aftershocks rattle in the night, but no more serious damage occurs.

At daylight, you and Ann pick your way through the debris-filled streets. You barely recognize the city. You have to scramble over fallen trees and jump over large cracks in the road.

You come across an ambulance crew. They are treating injured people.

"Can you let us know where we can find a shelter?" you ask. "I want to get in touch with my family."

"The school a couple of blocks down that way is an emergency shelter," says the emergency medical technician, pointing down the street. "Aid workers there will help you get in touch with your family."

At the shelter, workers have set up cots. A generator provides electricity.

They have cell phones that work. You wait in line to call your parents. They are safe. And so are you.

THE END

To follow another path, turn to page 123.
To read the conclusion, turn to page 211.

"I can drive to the hospital," you say. You and a few others help injured people into the van.

You have never seen such damage in your life. You dodge tree branches in the streets. In some areas, wide cracks have opened in the roadways. Every bump and jolt causes the injured people to scream in pain.

You groan as you come to an intersection that is completely blocked. You're only a short distance from the hospital. But you're stuck.

"We can't go any farther," you say. "Let me find some help. We're going to have to get you all to the hospital on foot."

In your hurry to get help, you step out of the van without looking at the ground. A downed power line is in the street, right in front of your foot. The jolt of electricity as you step on it stops your heart.

THE END

To follow another path, turn to page 123.
To read the conclusion, turn to page 211.

You start shaking from fear and adrenaline. You realize you're in no condition to drive. "I'll stay here," you say.

"Keep an eye on those people," the firefighter says to you, pointing to the injured people on the side of the road. "Let's keep them here. I don't want to take the chance of transporting them to the hospital. The roads likely are blocked by debris and dangerous. I've called other firefighting teams. More rescue workers will be on their way soon."

You stay with the injured people. Someone brings blankets from a nearby house. You keep the people warm and comfortable. About half an hour later, you hear sirens. The professional rescue workers have arrived. Emergency medical technicians, firefighters, and police officers attend to Tina and the rest of the injured people.

179

Turn the page.

After everyone is rescued and treated, you walk to a nearby shelter. You hope there will be a phone there that you can use to call Ann. A series of good decisions kept you safe and allowed you to help others as well.

THE END

To follow another path, turn to page 123.
To read the conclusion, turn to page 211.

"I'll go get him," you say.

"Be careful!" Ann says. "There could be an aftershock any minute."

You wave off her concerns. You head into the house and find George trapped in the bedroom. A heavy dresser fell onto his leg. You're just a few feet away from him when the house starts to shake again. It's an aftershock! The walls buckle and collapse around you. You fall down, and a piece of plaster falls on your head, killing you instantly.

THE END

To follow another path, turn to page 123.
To read the conclusion, turn to page 211.

"I'll go look for help," you say.

You run down the street as fast as you can, but the debris slows you down. A small aftershock ripples through the street. You lose your balance, but you're not hurt. You find a police officer at an intersection.

"Can you please help me? A friend is trapped in a house!"

The officer nods his head and calls for emergency workers on his radio. He follows you to Marge and George's house. By the time you get there, emergency workers arrive. They go into the house and return a few minutes later with George strapped to a stretcher. He is hurt, but alive. You made a good decision in leaving the rescue work to the professionals.

THE END

To follow another path, turn to page 123.
To read the conclusion, turn to page 211.

The American Red Cross helps victims of many types of disasters.

Sendai, Japan, is a city of about 1 million people.

CHAPTER 4

A Quake and a Big Wave

It's a beautiful Friday morning in the city of Sendai, Japan. You gaze at the bright blue sky through your office window. You are ready for the weekend after a hard week at work. You hear a knock at your door.

"Come in," you say, as you finish typing a report on your computer.

It's your boss, Ren Sato. He sits down across from you. "I would like you to go to Fukushima for the afternoon. We have an important client there who needs some help. I think you are the best person to help him."

Turn the page.

You sigh. You don't really want to go anywhere today. You promised your son that you would take him to a movie tonight.

"I know it is a last-minute request. I apologize," Mr. Sato says. "If you can't go, I will get someone else. But if you do it, I will appreciate it very much."

You want to keep your boss happy. But you've been looking forward to getting home, where your wife, Aiko, and son, Hideaki, wait.

To stay in Sendai, go to page 187.

To go to Fukushima, turn to page 189.

"I am going to stay here. But thank you for the offer," you tell Mr. Sato.

You finish typing your report just before lunchtime. You grab your briefcase and head to your car to pick up some lunch.

At a stoplight, your car begins to shake. Oh no, you think. This is a new car. It better not need repairs already.

But then your car begins to pitch and roll. It feels as if you're on a rollercoaster. Even with your seatbelt on, your body slams from side to side. Outside the car window, you see trees sway, utility poles topple, and power lines swing. Storefront windows explode, sending glass raining down into the street. It's an earthquake!

After several seconds the shaking stops. You get out of your car and see a group of frightened people gathered on the sidewalk. You join them.

Turn the page.

"What should we do now?" a woman asks.

"I think we should head to higher ground," replies a man. "Japan is surrounded by the ocean. This was a massive quake. I wouldn't be surprised if a tsunami is on its way."

"But how will we get anywhere?" says another woman. "The roads are destroyed. We'll have to leave on foot. I'm sure there will be aftershocks. Moving in this mess may be very dangerous."

To move to higher ground, turn to page **192**.

To stay on the street, turn to page **198**.

"I will go to Fukushima," you tell Mr. Sato. "Let me get my things."

After a train ride of a bit more than an hour, you arrive at your company's Fukushima office on the eighth floor of a high-rise building. You have just settled in when you feel a tremendous shaking. It's an earthquake!

You take shelter under a desk as you watch files, plants, and computers crash to the floor. The building creaks and roars. You think it might collapse. Screams and cries fill the air.

The trembling stops after a few moments. Your co-workers gather together and try to calm down.

"I think it's best that we leave," says one co-worker, Keiko. "We don't want to be in this building if aftershocks hit."

Turn the page.

After a few minutes of walking, you hear sirens. Ambulances and police cars pick their way carefully through the damaged streets. Rescue efforts are under way. At a street corner, a police officer directs traffic.

"Head to the nearest school, about two blocks that way." She points up the street. "The school was not damaged. You can get first aid there. Food and bottled water will arrive shortly."

At the shelter, you take a seat. Some people nearby are talking.

"I don't want to stay," one man says. "I'm sure the earthquake has damaged the nuclear reactors near the city. I'm going to leave as soon as possible."

"But where will you go? The roads are damaged," a woman tells him. "And more aftershocks may strike. You don't want to be on the road if that happens. We should listen to the aid workers here. They are telling people not to leave."

You want to get back to Sendai to check on your family. But Sendai is not safe. The city is on the coast of the Pacific Ocean and faces the threat of a tsunami. The man may be right about the damaged nuclear reactors. But trying to get home will not be a safe journey.

To head to Sendai, turn to page **195**.

To stay in Fukushima, turn to page **200**.

"Let's get moving," you say.

Your group heads to the part of the city located on the hilltop. At the top of a hill, you stop and listen. Besides the shouts and cries of people around you, you also hear a low rumbling. It sounds like a train.

The rumbling gets louder. You turn around and look back toward the coast. A huge black wall of water is headed toward you.

"It's a tsunami!" you yell. You're in front of a large building. A man in the doorway calls to you. "Come in here! We can go to the top floor. We'll be safest there!"

You all run into the building. You've never climbed stairs so quickly. You're almost to the top when the tsunami hits. The sound of the water hitting the building is deafening. A window near you shatters, cutting your skin.

Workers in Sendai scrambled to a factory roof to avoid the tsunami.

Turn the page.

After a few minutes everything becomes quiet. You've survived both an earthquake and a tsunami.

But you're bleeding badly from your cuts. You need to get help. Your cuts could become infected the longer you wait to go to a hospital. But you also need to find your wife and son. Your family has an emergency plan because you live in an earthquake zone. You agreed to go to the nearest shelter and stay there in case you were separated during an earthquake. If Aiko and Hideaki were looking for you, they would go to a shelter first.

To go to the shelter, turn to page **196.**

To find a hospital, turn to page **202.**

"Where are you headed?" you ask the man, whose name is Takumi. "I'm from Sendai and would like to get home as quickly as possible."

"I'm going to head inland," Takumi says. "I don't want to be anywhere near the coast for a while. But I heard some people over there say that they were going to Sendai." He points across the room. "I'll be happy to take you with me. I really think we'd all be safer if we go inland."

Takumi has a good point. You need to stay safe and healthy if you want to find your family. Sendai is likely still very dangerous. But you really want to make sure Aiko and Hideaki are OK.

To go to Sendai, turn to page 204.

To head inland, turn to page 205.

You bandage your cuts as best as you can with a first-aid kit you found in one of the offices. A cut on your left arm is very deep and will need stitches.

You walk out of the building with your group. The street is covered with several inches of water. The cold, dirty seawater soaks your shoes and pants. You trip on debris and fall to the street. The salty water stings your cuts. Emergency sirens are blaring as rescue attempts begin. The city comes back to life as rescue crews try to help survivors.

There's a police car at the end of the block. "Excuse me," you say to the officer. "Where is the nearest shelter?"

"There's a school five blocks to the west," the officer says. "Go there and wait for help."

You make your way to the school. You begin to shiver, and your cuts are still bleeding. You start to feel dizzy and faint. First-aid workers help you to a chair. They wash your cuts and put new bandages on them.

You know you're supposed to stay at a shelter according to your family's emergency plan. But what if Aiko and Hideaki are trapped in your house and can't get to a shelter?

To go to the house, turn to page 207.

To stay at the shelter, turn to page 209.

You wait on the street. One co-worker, Yoko, has deep cuts on her legs from flying glass. She can't walk, and you don't want to leave her.

Just then, the earth starts to shake again. You all grab one another and hang on. The aftershock is less severe than the earthquake, but you're still frightened. After it's over, you sit on the curb.

"What's that noise?" says one of the men. It sounds like a low rumbling, like a train. The ground shakes ever so slightly. There's a hill nearby. You scramble up the hillside and look toward the sea.

What you see frightens you to your very core. Past the beach, you see what looks like a moving, swirling, black wall. It comes closer and closer. It's a tsunami, and there's no escape. "The water is coming!" you scream. "Everyone, move higher!

You and your co-workers try to get up the hill, but Yoko slows you down. The roar of the huge wave fills your ears.

In March 2011 a massive earthquake triggered a tsunami in Japan.

Within moments, the water crashes around you. You hang on to a tree trunk with all your might. You hold your breath as the water hits you like a liquid brick wall. You cling desperately to the tree, but the force of the water tears you away. You are one of thousands the tsunami claims that day.

THE END

To follow another path, turn to page 123.
To read the conclusion, turn to page 211.

It's best to stay at the shelter until you learn if the roads are safe. You are talking to some people a few hours later when the rescue workers make an announcement.

"We just learned that the Fukushima nuclear plant is seriously damaged. We need to evacuate everything in a 12-mile radius. We have arranged transportation to shelters a few miles away. Stay inside until the buses arrive. You will be exposed to less radiation if you stay inside the building."

You can't see the radiation from the nuclear plant, but you know it's out there. Even indoors, you feel at risk. You should have left when you had the chance.

You arrive at the new shelter. After a couple of days, you are able to make it back home to Sendai and are reunited with your family. But the radiation has long-lasting effects that won't show up for several years. You survived the earthquake, but your health is permanently damaged because of that day in Fukushima.

THE END

To follow another path, turn to page 123.
To read the conclusion, turn to page 211.

You walk outside. Several inches of dirty, cold seawater fill the streets. After taking a few steps, you stumble. The dirty water washes over your wounds.

The sounds of sirens fill the air. Rescue efforts are under way. A police officer stands on the corner.

"Do you know if the hospital is open?" you ask.

"Yes. It was damaged, but they are treating patients there."

You head to the hospital, where they give you antibiotics. You are at a high risk of infection because of the dirty water entering your wounds.

"You made a good decision to get treated right away," the doctor says. "I think we will see some very serious illnesses within a couple of days. Many people are badly injured."

At the hospital, you put your name on a list of survivors. The list will go to many shelters so people can check on loved ones.

After a few hours, you get a welcome surprise. It's Aiko and Hideaki! They saw your name on a list and came to find you. You have survived the earthquake and tsunami with your health and family intact.

THE END

To follow another path, turn to page 123.
To read the conclusion, turn to page 211.

You find the people heading to Sendai. They agree to take you with them.

"Let's take the back roads," the driver, Hana, says. "I'm sure they have shut down the highways already."

You head out of town. Very few cars are on the road. You have to travel slowly because the roads are badly damaged. A few miles out of Fukushima, you feel a rumbling. The van pitches and rolls.

"It's an aftershock!" Hana screams.

You hit your head on the window. The road buckles in front of you and sends the van spinning into the ditch. The van rolls over and lands upside down. You hear moans from the other passengers before everything goes black. The car crash has taken your life.

THE END

To follow another path, turn to page 123.
To read the conclusion, turn to page 211.

"I think you're right," you tell Takumi. "Let's go inland."

You walk a few blocks to Takumi's house, even though you know going outside puts you at a high risk of radiation exposure. But you want to get out of town as soon as possible. At Takumi's house, you both get into his car. The roads directly outside of Fukushima are heavily damaged, and you must travel slowly. But the farther inland you go, the better the roads are. Several miles away from Fukushima, you notice the damage in the country is much less.

You decide to stop in a town about 50 miles away. At a small café, you see a young woman with a computer.

"Excuse me, could I borrow your computer?" you ask her. "I just came from Fukushima, and I want to try to contact my wife in Sendai. I left my cell phone at the office."

Turn the page.

"I just read that someone has set up a people finder online," she says. "You could type in your name and say that you're OK."

You find the site and type in your information. A few hours later, you check back in. Thankfully, Aiko posted a message! She and Hideaki are OK. You leave her a message to come to you, where she and Hideaki will be safe. You will find a place to stay here until it is safe to return to your home in Sendai.

THE END

To follow another path, turn to page 123.
To read the conclusion, turn to page 211.

Your house is about a 15-minute walk away. You wade through streets flooded with water and debris. You trip several times, and your bandages work loose. Water gets into your cuts. But you must get home and check on your family.

When you get to the house, no one is there. You can only hope that Aiko and Hideaki have gone to a shelter. You probably should have stayed there.

You are shocked at the devastation you see. Several inches of water cover the first floor. Dishes have tumbled out of the cabinets. Food from your pantry is spilled onto the floor. Upstairs, furniture is tipped over. Your television fell to the floor during the quake and is smashed. Cracks appear in the walls.

You head back to the shelter to find your family. But your cuts are still bleeding heavily. You start to feel weak and dizzy. You make it through the shelter doors and then collapse.

Turn the page.

When you wake up, you are at the hospital. You are in pain, but you are relieved to see Aiko and Hideaki at your bedside.

"You have been in a coma for several days," Aiko said. "An infection settled into your legs. Doctors had to amputate your left foot in order to save your life."

You have survived. But your decision to leave the shelter when you did has changed your life forever.

THE END

To follow another path, turn to page 123.
To read the conclusion, turn to page 211.

You decide it would be best to stay here and wait for Aiko and Hideaki. A doctor looks at your wounds. "I'm going to start you on antibiotics," she says. "Your cuts were exposed to seawater, which is full of bacteria. You could get a serious infection."

You take the medicine and fall asleep. When you wake up, you look for Aiko and Hideaki, but they still are not here. A rescue worker puts your name on a list. The list will be sent to all the shelters to help reunite families. After two days of stress and worry, a rescue worker says to you, "Your wife and son are safe. They are at a shelter a few miles away. They will be here soon."

When Aiko and Hideaki arrive, you all get on a bus to the city where your parents live. After a series of good decisions, you have all survived.

THE END

To follow another path, turn to page 123.
To read the conclusion, turn to page 211.

An 8.8-magnitude earthquake destroyed a road in Chile in 2010.

CHAPTER 5

Surviving an Earthquake

Do you have what it takes to survive an earthquake? Earthquake survivors are alert and prepared. They know where danger lurks. Inside buildings, familiar objects such as unsecured furniture and electronics can become deadly missiles. Trees and power lines outdoors pose threats. Bridges and overpasses may collapse. And at the beach, a tsunami can sweep away everything in its path.

A pre-earthquake plan can help you make good decisions when disaster strikes. Find the places in every room where you can drop, cover, and hold on. Get first-aid and CPR training.

Turn the page.

You and your family members also should choose a meeting place in case you get separated. Even if your house appears to be safe after an earthquake, you should plan to seek safe shelter elsewhere. Natural gas leaks and other invisible threats in your home can be present for days or weeks after a quake.

The last thing you want to do is to scramble for important items such as shoes and flashlights during an earthquake. A packed disaster kit will save valuable time and may even save your life.

If you have to go to a shelter, what should you bring? The U.S. Geological Survey recommends bringing the following items with you to a shelter:

- Your own bottled water, food, and snacks.

- Items for sleeping, such as a pillow, blankets, and an air mattress or pad.

- Any needed medicines.

- Extra clothes, including warm clothes such as jackets.

- Bathroom supplies, such as a towel, washcloth, toothpaste, and toothbrush.

- Identification and insurance information.

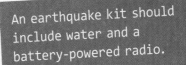

An earthquake kit should include water and a battery-powered radio.

Most emergency shelters don't allow pets, so you will need to have a plan in place for your pet as well. These items should be part of that plan:

- Find out if there is an emergency shelter where you can take your pet in case of a disaster.

- Keep your pet up to date on its vaccinations.

- Make sure your pet wears a collar with your name, address, and phone number on it, or have your pet microchipped.

Once you are able to return to your home, you must concentrate on getting your life back in order. This process can be more stressful than the earthquake itself. People need time to heal from the massive changes an earthquake can cause. It can be weeks before power is restored and clean drinking water is available. Buildings you are used to seeing might be destroyed. You may have to find other ways to get around because of damaged roads.

Most of all, earthquake survival depends on staying calm. You must be prepared and make smart decisions based on what you know about earthquakes and their dangers. Many people have survived major earthquakes. With the right knowledge and decisions, you can be one of them.

REAL SURVIVORS

Miracle Baby

One of the tiniest survivors of the March 11, 2011, Japanese earthquake and tsunami was a 4-month-old baby girl. She was swept away from her parents when the tsunami waters flooded their house in Ishinomaki. For three days, her parents thought she was dead. But rescue workers heard a cry in the rubble and found her. No one knows how she survived the damage, but she proved that miracles can occur even amid disaster.

Alaska Survivor

Eleven-year-old Paul Timothy "Timmy" Selanoff was walking along the shore near Chenega, Alaska, on March 27, 1964, when a huge earthquake struck. Timmy dodged quaking boulders as he ran for safety on top of a cliff. There he watched massive tsunami waves wipe out his village. All that was left was the school. Twenty-six people from Chenega died that day— one-quarter of the village's population. The victims included Tommy's brother and sister.

Trapped in Rubble

When a 7.0 magnitude earthquake struck the Caribbean nation of Haiti on January 12, 2010, many people were trapped in collapsed buildings. One of those trapped was 47-year-old American Rick Santos. He and four co-workers were in the lobby of the Hotel Montana in the city of Port-au-Prince when it collapsed around them. They were trapped for three nights, but were protected by the lobby's huge front desk. The only food they had was one lollipop, which they shared. Santos and two co-workers were rescued and survived. The two other co-workers died.

Deadly Tsunami

When a massive underwater earthquake struck off the coast of Indonesia on December 26, 2004, it unleashed a tsunami that killed more than 200,000 people. TV host Nate Berkus was vacationing on Sri Lanka with his friend Fernando Bengoechea. The two were in a small hut near the shore when the tsunami hit. Berkus and Bengoechea were washed out in the swirling waters. Berkus managed to swim to a fence and climb to a rooftop, where he was safe. Bengoechea was never found and is believed dead.

SURVIVAL QUIZ

1. The safest place to be during an earthquake is:
   a. On a bridge.
   b. On a sidewalk next to a tall building.
   c. Underneath a piece of sturdy furniture, such as a table.
   d. Outside near a large tree.

2. Earthquakes are more likely in the Ring of Fire, which surrounds this ocean:
   a. Pacific Ocean
   b. Atlantic Ocean
   c. Indian Ocean
   d. Arctic Ocean

3. This scale is used to measure the strength of earthquakes:
   a. Mighty Scale
   b. Smith Scale
   c. Richter Scale
   d. Big Scale

Answers: C, A, C

Can You Survive

THE

JUNGLE?

An Interactive Survival Adventure

by Matt Doeden

Consultant:
Jim Penn
Associate Professor
Department of Geography and Planning
Grand Valley State University

TABLE OF CONTENTS

About Your Adventure.................................223

Chapter 1
Lost in the Jungle 225

Chapter 2
On the Move 231

Chapter 3
Making Camp...257

Chapter 4
In Search of Maria....................................285

Chapter 5
Surviving the Jungle...............................319

Real Survivors 324
Survival Quiz 326

About Your
ADVENTURE

YOU are lost in a dangerous place—the Amazon jungle. Predators prowl through the thick vegetation. Deadly snakes and spiders creep in dark places. Huge black caimans and electric eels lurk below murky waters. How will you survive?

In this book you'll deal with extreme survival situations. You'll explore how the knowledge you have and the choices you make can mean the difference between life and death.

Chapter One sets the scene. Then you choose which path to read. Follow the directions at the bottom of each page. The choices you make will change your outcome. After you finish one path, go back and read the others for new experiences and more adventures.

YOU CHOOSE the path you
take through your adventure.

Small planes are often the only way to access remote areas of the world.

Lost in the Jungle

You throw your backpack over your shoulder and wave to your parents before stepping aboard the small airplane. It's the end of summer vacation—time to head back to civilization and school.

You've spent an exciting summer living in the basin of the Amazon River in South America—the largest rain forest in the world. Your parents are photographers working on a book about the Amazon's huge variety of life. You've spent all summer in the hot, sticky jungle helping them find interesting plants, animals, and insects. You've even taken some photos with your own camera.

Turn the page.

But now the camera is tucked away in your backpack, along with your journal. You also brought a change of clothes, your trusty pocketknife, a bag of trail mix, and a bottle of water. The excitement of trekking through the Amazon with your parents is over. You wish you could finish the job with them, but they won't let you miss school.

You take your seat behind Maria, the airplane's pilot. She will fly you to Brazil's capital city, Brasilia. There you'll board a jet headed for home. You talk as the plane takes off, telling Maria about your adventures. But soon you close your eyes and drift off to sleep.

Suddenly you're awakened from a dream. The airplane is shuddering. You sit forward, startled. The plane's engine is making a horrible coughing noise. You can feel the plane descending.

"Chute!" Maria shouts, pointing to the back. "Put on your parachute! We're going down!"

You quickly grab one of the parachutes and begin strapping it to your back. You've done this before but never for a real emergency. Your fingers tremble as you work the straps, but you manage to put it on. You grab the other parachute and hand it to Maria, but she waves it away.

"Go!" she shouts. "There's no time! I'll try to find an open spot to land!"

You grab your backpack and do as you're told. You pull the door open. With only a small hesitation, you jump. As soon as you're clear of the plane, you pull your parachute's cord. The chute pops open, slowing your fall with a jolt. You turn and watch as the plane goes down in the distance.

Turn the page.

A parachute can carry you for many miles.

Your landing is rough. You're scraped and bruised from falling through the canopy of trees. Still, you were lucky. You're on the ground and alive. You wonder what happened to Maria. The plane was headed south. You look in that direction. From the jungle floor, you can't see more than 20 feet ahead.

Slowly, the reality of your situation hits you. You're alone and lost in the jungle. You're certain there will be a rescue search. But the Amazon is huge. You can't just sit around and hope to be rescued. As you see it, you have three choices.

To take off in search of rescue, turn to page **231**.

To build a camp and try to signal rescuers, turn to page **257**.

To look for the plane and Maria, turn to page **285**.

It's easy to lose your direction in the green tangle of the jungle.

CHAPTER 2

On the Move

You've had some training in jungle survival. The best chance of finding rescue is to head downhill. Most villages lie along waterways. Water flows downhill, so that's the direction you should go.

There's no time to waste. Every minute you spend in the jungle alone is a minute of danger. You choose a direction that seems to be downhill and start moving.

The jungle is thick. You find a stick to clear away plants and branches as you move. The air is hot, humid, and filled with mosquitoes and other biting insects. Before long your water is gone. The ground is wet and muddy in many places, but there is no clear water available. You keep the empty water bottle, hoping to fill it up later.

Turn the page.

After hours of walking, you come upon a stream. It's not much—just a few feet wide—but it's something to follow. The stream's water looks clean. Your throat is dry, and you know that your body desperately needs water.

You fill your empty water bottle but hesitate before taking a drink. The water could contain tiny organisms that will make you sick. If you drink the water now, you could keep moving until sunset. Otherwise, you'd have to build a fire, heat the water to kill any dangerous organisms, and camp here for the night.

To drink the water now and keep moving, go to page 233.

To build a fire, heat the water, and camp here, turn to page 236.

You're starting to feel dizzy. You need water right away. You remember a trick you saw on TV where someone used T-shirt material as a crude water filter. You wrap layers of your T-shirt around the mouth of the bottle and let the water pass through it. You don't know if it will make a difference, but it couldn't hurt.

You take a deep breath and drink. The water is warm but refreshing. You find yourself gulping it down. You empty the bottle and refill it. Now you're ready to keep going.

You follow the stream down, knowing that it will likely lead to a larger river. An hour or two later, that's exactly what you find. The stream empties into a river that's at least 50 feet wide. You're thrilled to have found a major waterway. By following this river, you're likely to find people.

Turn the page.

Even water that looks clean can contain dangerous organisms.

But the sun is starting to set. You'll have to camp for the night. You have little time to build a proper shelter. You gather some branches and drape leaves over the top. You build the shelter up and away from the river. A rainstorm could cause a flash flood, so you need to keep some distance from the water.

It's a rough night of sleep. You're uncomfortable. You constantly feel things crawling on you. Late in the night, you're gripped by terrible stomach cramps and diarrhea. It must have been the water.

By daybreak you feel awful. The idea of fighting through the jungle, the heat, and the humidity is almost too much. You're not sure you can move far without passing out. All you want to do is lie in the shade and wait for someone to find you.

To get up and continue searching for rescue, turn to page **239**.

To stay and hope someone finds you, turn to page **241**.

Drinking water straight out of a jungle stream could be a terrible mistake, no matter how thirsty you are. Instead you use the remaining hours of daylight to build a shelter and a fire. The shelter is just a simple lean-to built with sticks and branches and covered with leaves.

To build a fire, you gather small sticks and any other dry material you can find, including some pages from your journal. You remove the lens of your camera. The powerful lens focuses the sun's light to a small point. This creates intense heat, which lights the paper and starts the fire.

Carefully you build the small flame into a roaring blaze. Next you use one of your shoelaces to tie the water bottle to a stick propped above the fire. The bottle is high enough above the flame that the plastic won't melt but close enough to heat the water. You know that the water doesn't have to boil to be purified. It only needs to get hot enough to kill any bacteria or parasites living in it.

Encircling a fire with rocks helps keep it contained.

Soon you're gulping clean, safe water. You refill the bottle and repeat the process so you have more water for tomorrow.

After munching some trail mix, you lie down for the night. You don't sleep much, but aside from nagging insects, nothing disturbs your little shelter.

Turn the page.

At daybreak you take off again. You follow the stream downhill to where it joins a river. The river is fairly large, with what looks like a strong current. A raft might carry you downstream quickly. But you would risk running into a caiman, anaconda, or other water predator. You then see what appears to be a trail of smoke far off in the distance, upstream from the river. The smoke could be coming from a village, but it might be miles away.

To travel by foot upstream, turn to page 242.

To build a raft and try to float downriver, turn to page 244.

The last thing you want to do right now is to get up and start moving again. But you know that if you give up now, you're dead. Your stomach is full of harmful bacteria or parasites, and you don't have much time. You must use what little strength you have to search for rescue.

You move back toward the river. With luck, you'll find a village downstream.

Turn the page.

As you stumble weakly along the riverbank, you notice a large log near the water's edge. You might be able to roll it into the water and use it to ride the current. That would get you downstream a lot faster. But it's also a risk. You might not have the strength to hold onto the log, especially if the current is strong. Or you could become caiman bait.

To try using the log to float down the river, turn to page 247.

To continue on foot, turn to page 249.

You feel terrible. The water you drank must have been loaded with bacteria and parasites. They're churning in your stomach now, making you too sick to do much of anything.

You lie down in your makeshift shelter. Later in the morning, a rain shower passes through. You know you should try to collect some of the fresh rainwater, but you don't have the energy.

Over the rest of the day, you grow weaker. By nightfall you're drifting in and out of consciousness. All you can do is hope that rescuers can somehow find you here. But in your heart, you know that's not going to happen.

THE END

To follow another path, turn to page 229.
To read the conclusion, turn to page 319.

Smoke could mean people, so that's the direction you go. You sling your backpack over your shoulder and start walking. After an hour or so, you notice the riverbanks are steeper and rockier. You also begin to hear a faint rumbling.

Soon you realize why. You look up to see a waterfall straight ahead of you.

"Oh no," you mumble to yourself.

The river crashes down over a small wall of rock. This cliff extends to both sides of the river, forming a barrier. You're not willing to double back and find another way around. That would take far too long.

You notice a spot where the rock face is sloped more gently. It looks like you could try climbing it. But without a rope, any slip could mean disaster. If you want to continue upstream toward the smoke trail, though, it's your only choice.

Maybe going downstream was the better idea after all. You could build a raft to help make up some of the time you lost following the smoke on foot.

To build a raft and go downstream, turn to page **244**.

To try to climb the rock wall, turn to page **251**.

You set down your backpack and get to work. The jungle provides you with everything you need to build a raft. You snap off tree limbs and small tree trunks and line them up. Next you collect some of the vines that grow all over the Amazon's trees. You strip the vines of their leaves and soak them in river water. The wet vines make great rope.

You use the vines to tie together the wood that forms the base of your raft. The project takes most of the day. A late-morning rain shower cools you off and provides some fresh drinking water.

Soon your raft is finished. It's not strong enough to survive any rapids, so you'll need a way to steer to shore if you come upon some. You grab a long stick to push yourself downriver and to steer when needed.

Late in the afternoon, you launch the raft and climb aboard. It supports your weight. Water seeps up through the cracks, but the raft keeps your body out of the water and away from predators. You push yourself out to the middle of the river and let the current take you. Soon you're floating downriver at a good pace. You're tired, hungry, and thirsty, but you're moving.

Not long after you've started, you spot something ahead. A large black caiman sits in the shallow water along one of the banks. He's watching you.

Turn the page.

Caimans are fast swimmers. You have no doubt he could easily catch you before you pass by. Your heart races as the reptile slowly begins moving in your direction.

Male black caimans can grow to more than 13 feet long.

To use your pole to head for land on the opposite river bank, turn to page 253.

To continue downriver, turn to page 254.

Getting into a river with nothing but a log is a terrible risk. But you're sick, and time is not on your side. If you're going to survive, you have to take big risks.

The log is heavy, but you manage to roll it into the river. The current is weaker at the river's edge, so you walk the log out to waist-deep water. You try to climb onto the log, but it won't support your weight. You'll just have to hold onto it. You don't like leaving your lower body dangling in unfamiliar waters, but you have little choice.

In the middle of the river, the current is stronger. You cling to the log and watch as the jungle goes by. Within just a few minutes, you're already far from your starting place. It would have taken you hours to travel the same distance by foot.

By afternoon a blistering sun beats down on you. You're dizzy and having trouble concentrating. Your body is still fighting whatever bacteria or parasites you drank, but it's losing the fight. All you can think about is holding onto the log.

Your river soon joins with a larger river. And then you hear voices. You look up and can hardly believe your eyes—you see a boat! Weakly, you try to signal the people aboard, but they've already spotted you. A man throws a life preserver in your direction.

You let go of the log and grab the life preserver. You've made it! You're still very sick, but you know that with some medical help, you'll make a full recovery.

THE END

To follow another path, turn to page 229.
To read the conclusion, turn to page 319.

Travel by foot may be slow and tiring, but at least you won't be at the mercy of a wild river. You fight your way through the heavy vegetation on the riverbank. Rain begins to fall. You collect some rainwater as it drips down from the canopy of trees above. At least this water is pure. You drink a little but vomit it up just a few minutes later.

Your pace is slowing. Painful stomach cramps make you stop and double over several times. Fighting through the jungle is hard work, and you just don't have the strength to do it.

By the afternoon, the sun is beating down mercilessly on your skin. You keep moving, unwilling to give up. But your body is failing. The heat is too much. Darkness is creeping around the edges of your vision. Your head feels light. Too late, you realize that you're about to faint.

Turn the page.

Slowly the world comes back into focus. You realize you must have fainted and hit your head, which is slick with blood. You're not entirely sure where you are. Weakly, you call out to your parents. You can't understand why they don't answer.

Your head feels like it's spinning. You close your eyes. You tell yourself that it's just for a moment. But part of you understands that you won't be opening them again.

THE END

To follow another path, turn to page 229.
To read the conclusion, turn to page 319.

You start up the cliff, finding handholds and footholds in the sharp, jagged rock. The rocks are also wet and slippery, so you have to be careful with each move.

Slowly you work your way up the rock face. You're more than halfway there, and now you can use exposed tree roots as handholds. You grab onto a root and use it to pull yourself up. But as you lunge up with one foot, the root snaps off in your hand. Desperately, you grab for another handhold, but it's too late.

You hit the rock below with a sickening crunch. You black out momentarily from the pain. Sometime later you regain consciousness. You can't feel one arm and know it must be broken. You can see a jagged piece of bone jutting out of one leg. And the back of your head is matted with blood.

Turn the page.

Somehow you survived the fall. But with several broken bones and a head injury, you know that your survival will be short-lived. You took a risk, and you're going to pay the ultimate price. With your one working arm, you reach into your pack for your journal and pen and scrawl, "Good-bye."

THE END

To follow another path, turn to page 229.
To read the conclusion, turn to page 319.

Black caimans are lightning-quick in the water, so you think you have a better chance on land. Frantically you push yourself to the opposite shore. Your raft scrapes against the river bottom. You step off, pulling the raft behind you. You look over your shoulder. The huge reptile is still on the opposite shore. It's no longer watching you.

Relieved, you take a deep breath. That's when you notice a flash of motion out of the corner of your eye.

You didn't stop to think that where there's one black caiman, there might be more. In your panic you've steered almost right into the jaws of another caiman. The attack happens so quickly that you barely have time to regret your decision.

THE END

To follow another path, turn to page 229.
To read the conclusion, turn to page 319.

For all you know, there could be another caiman on the opposite shore. All you can do is continue. You hold your breath as the huge reptile slips below the water's surface. Your heart races. Your hands are shaking. Where is it? It could be right below your raft.

A minute passes. Then another. Your heartbeat slows. The caiman isn't coming after you. Perhaps it wasn't hungry. Or maybe the raft didn't look like food from below. Either way, you're alive and you're safe—for now.

The river soon flows into a still larger river. The sun is getting low in the sky, but you want to go just a bit farther before pulling to shore.

You're rewarded for your determination. In the distance, you see faint lights. The current carries you toward a small village. Several men are fishing on the riverbank.

"Help!" you shout to them. Two of the men jump into their boat and row to you. They pull you to safety. The villagers have a small two-way radio that you use to contact the police. You tell them to send rescuers immediately to search for Maria and the crashed airplane.

You've made it. You've survived the Amazon and all of its dangers. And what a story you'll have to tell your friends at home!

THE END

To follow another path, turn to page 229.
To read the conclusion, turn to page 319.

Caves and crevices can offer some protection from the weather.

CHAPTER 3

Making Camp

It won't be long before someone realizes your plane is missing. Maria filed a flight plan with the national aviation authority. That means rescuers will have an idea of where to look for you. The best thing you can do is to find a place to build a shelter. When rescuers come, you'll be ready.

To the west, the ground slopes upward. You want to camp on high ground. Heavy rains are frequent in the Amazon, and you never know where a flash flood might occur. High ground will be at much lower risk. Signaling rescuers will be easier from there too.

Turn the page.

You fold your parachute and sling it over your right shoulder. Its weight will slow you down, but it might be useful in building a shelter.

Mosquitoes and other insects swarm around you as you move through the jungle. You step carefully. A venomous snake could be waiting under any fallen log. The sounds of the jungle surround you—buzzing insects, jumping fish, and rustling leaves.

Piranhas are a danger in Amazon waters. These fish have razor-sharp teeth.

After about an hour, you come upon several large boulders. They form a small clearing in the jungle. This might be as good a spot for a camp as you'll find.

It's now late afternoon. There's much to do before sunset. You'll need a sturdy shelter to protect you from the weather. But you'll also need food and water. You've already gone through most of your water. You'll need to find another water source quickly.

To build a shelter, turn to page 260.

To search for food and water, turn to page 262.

Shelter is your top priority. You've still got your bag of trail mix. That can be your meal for the night.

This is where dragging your parachute through the jungle will pay off. You find two small trees about 10 feet apart. With your knife, you cut several of the cords on the parachute. After tying them together, you tie each end to one of the trees. Next you cut away a section of the parachute fabric. You drape this over the cords and then secure the ends to the ground. This forms a crude A-shaped tent. It isn't much to look at, but it will keep you dry at night.

Then you gather several medium-sized, straight branches. You lay them down in your shelter for a makeshift bed. The branches won't get you far off the ground, but they might keep away some of the insects crawling along the jungle floor.

You're exhausted by the time the shelter is finished. The sun is quickly setting. You try to start a fire by rubbing sticks together, but you get nowhere. So you go to bed without a fire and put up with the merciless mosquito attack. It's a long and miserable night, but it could be much worse.

The next morning you grab your pocketknife and head out into the jungle. You find an inga tree with some nearly ripe fruit. You gulp the delicious fruit hungrily.

261

Turn to page **274.**

All that walking has made you hungry, and you want to keep up your strength. You set down your backpack and head back into the jungle. You know that buriti palm fruits, sweet inga fruits, and other fruits grow naturally in the Amazon.

Buriti palms produce small fruit with scaled skins.

As you move through the jungle, you carefully watch all around you. You come across a trampled area that looks like some sort of animal trail. There are tracks in the mud alongside the trail. You're not sure, but they look like peccary tracks. If you could kill a peccary, you'd have food to last you many days. But hunting is a risky choice. Peccaries can easily injure or kill a person.

To continue to forage for fruit, turn to page 264.

To hunt for a peccary, turn to page 267.

Your mouth waters at the thought of freshly roasted meat, but you decide against hunting. You'd have to use a lot of energy with no guarantee of getting your prey. Even if you did kill an animal, cooking it over an open fire might attract jaguars.

The jungle offers plenty of food with less risk. If you can't find fruit, you can always turn to beetle grubs. You've seen survival experts eat them on TV. They look disgusting, but you're willing to do whatever it takes to survive.

Luckily you don't have to resort to eating grubs. You find a stand of buriti palm trees. One palm has dropped fruit that's almost ripe. You collect several pieces of fruit. You use your knife to peel off the tough, scaly outer covering, so you can eat the yellow flesh. The half-ripe fruit tastes great.

The sun is nearing the horizon, so you head back to camp. There's no time to build a proper shelter or a fire. Instead you wrap yourself up in your parachute. It's a long, miserable night. With no fire or proper shelter, the mosquitoes are relentless. You sleep very little and wake up sore and tired.

You're not going to spend another night like that. It's time to build a shelter. You run some of the cord from your parachute between two trees. Then you drape your parachute cloth over it, forming a crude tent. Now you've got shelter and food. Things are looking up.

Turn to page 274.

You can't resist the idea of grilling meat over a campfire. You find a long branch and sharpen the end with your knife, making a crude spear. With the spear in hand, you quietly follow the tracks.

After several minutes you hear a rustling up ahead. Something large is moving in the dense vegetation. It might be the peccary. You move forward carefully.

Suddenly the rustling stops. Your prey has heard you. You charge forward. But whatever it is you're chasing darts away under the cover of the jungle.

To continue your chase, go to page 267.

To give up and return to camp, turn to page 269.

You follow, unwilling to give up. You dash through the jungle. Leaves, branches, and vines whack you in the face. Suddenly you find yourself sprawling forward. Your foot has caught on a root. You crash onto the ground, opening a wide gash in your head.

Turn the page.

You black out for a moment. When you regain consciousness, there's a sharp, throbbing pain in your right leg. You look down to see your ankle wrenched at an awful angle. You try to move it but almost black out again from the pain.

Your ankle is broken. You can't walk or even stand. You're lying alone in a thick jungle. You have no food, no water, no supplies, and no shelter. And worst of all, you have no hope.

You feel suddenly tired. You're losing lots of blood, and your body was already dehydrated. You know if you close your eyes, you may never open them again.

You fight to stay conscious. But you've lost too much blood. It's a fight you won't win.

THE END

To follow another path, turn to page 229.
To read the conclusion, turn to page 319.

You know better than to go running after unknown prey in the jungle. You tried to get meat, but you failed. It's time to head back and work on your shelter.

Peccaries are less than 3 feet long and can weigh more than 60 pounds.

You start heading back the way you came, but after a few minutes, nothing looks familiar. The sun is quickly setting, so you know which direction is west. But your camp isn't where you thought it would be.

You double back again. With every turn you get more lost and confused. The sky is growing darker and darker. Soon you can barely see more than a few feet in front of you. You're desperate to find your camp. But in the dark, you might only get more confused. Maybe you should climb a tree and spend the night here, off the ground.

To climb a tree for the night, go to page 271.

To continue your search in the dark, turn to page 272.

There's nothing more you can do in the dark. It's time to get off the ground and out of reach of predators. You find a solid tree branch and pull yourself up. You don't dare fall asleep. But at least you're not on the damp ground, surrounded by snakes, spiders, and other creatures.

At sunrise, you lower yourself to the jungle floor. You think your camp is to the west, so you head in the direction opposite of the sun. Within 20 minutes, you reach your camp. You plop down on the ground and munch on some trail mix. Then you start work on a shelter. You're not spending another night without one.

Turn to page 274.

Your camp has to be around here somewhere. You just have to keep searching.

After about 20 minutes, the jungle is completely dark. You fumble along through the brush, feeling your way more than seeing. You stumble over a tree root, sprawling to the ground. You try crawling, but as you put your right hand forward, you feel a sharp, hot pain in your wrist.

You jerk your arm back. Something bit you, probably a snake. You stand, wiping the tears from your face. Your wrist feels strange. It pulses and starts to feel numb. Soon the feeling spreads farther up your arm.

The bite was venomous. Clutching your chest, you fall to your knees. You can't breathe. You gasp, but your lungs won't take any air. You black out and fall to the jungle floor. That's where you die, alone in the jungle.

The tree boa can inflict a painful bite.

THE END

To follow another path, turn to page 229.
To read the conclusion, turn to page 319.

Later in the morning, a rain shower passes through. You collect water as it drips down your parachute. You fill your bottle to the brim.

The Amazon averages more than 7 feet of rain each year.

You consider your priorities. You have food, shelter, and some water. Now you need to figure out a way to signal any rescuers. You expect airplanes and helicopters will be looking for you and Maria.

Your camp is in a natural clearing, so that will help. You just need a way to get the rescuers' attention. You could spell out the word "HELP" with wood and branches. But what are the odds that rescuers would see it?

The other option is to build a signal fire. You'd need a big blaze with lots of smoke. You're not sure you can build such a big fire by yourself.

*To prepare a signal fire, turn to page **276**.*

*To use wood to spell out a cry for help, turn to page **277**.*

You start by collecting the driest wood you can find. You arrange three large pieces in a pyramid. This will form the base of your fire. Underneath, you add smaller branches and pages from your journal as kindling.

The drier wood will burn hot, but it won't create a lot of smoke. You need green, wet wood and vegetation for that. You use your pocketknife to cut living branches off nearby trees. These branches are full of moisture. Finally you add a layer of green leaves and vegetation. They will burn slowly, but they'll release huge amounts of smoke.

Your fire is ready to light by late afternoon.

*To light the fire now, turn to page **279**.*

*To wait until you hear an aircraft, turn to page **282**.*

You imagine rescuers seeing a huge "HELP" from the air. There would be no mistaking that message because Brazilian pilots are trained to communicate in basic English. You collect long branches, carefully laying them out to form each letter. Soon you're dripping with sweat from dragging heavy wood around. But by the time you're done, you're pleased with your signal. Now you just need someone to see it.

Late that afternoon, you hear something from above. It's the sound of distant helicopter blades. It must be the search-and-rescue team!

You hurry to the clearing, shouting and waving your arms. But the hum of the helicopter soon fades away. It returns later, but it never comes close.

Turn the page.

Several times during the next few days you hear the sound of an aircraft. It never comes close enough to spot your sign. Then the sounds stop. The search has probably ended. You realize that from the air your sign would hardly be noticeable in the dense jungle.

No one is going to find you here. You get ready to start walking. You're weak and tired. You're not sure you'll make it far. But it's the only chance you have. You won't stop fighting.

THE END

To follow another path, turn to page 229.
To read the conclusion, turn to page 319.

There's no telling when rescuers might come. You have got to send your signal now. You can always build another signal fire later if nobody spots this one.

You pull your camera from your backpack and carefully remove the lens. The lens is a powerful way to focus the sun's rays onto a single point. You focus the sunlight onto some tinder. In a few seconds, the tinder begins to smoke and catches fire. You carefully tend the flame, helping it to spread.

Within a few minutes, the fire's base is burning. It takes a lot longer before the wet vegetation starts to burn. But when it does, it releases big, billowing plumes of smoke. The smoke rises above the jungle canopy.

Turn the page.

You continue to feed the fire, adding both wood and green vegetation to keep the smoke coming. As you're trudging through the jungle looking for more wood, you hear something in the distance.

You rush to the clearing. The noise is getting louder. You let out a shout as you realize it's a helicopter. Your signal fire has worked!

Helicopter rescues are made more difficult by the lack of open areas in dense rain forests.

You're going to be rescued! You will have the helicopter pilot search for Maria too.

The jungle can be a scary, deadly place. But you stayed calm and remained focused on the goal of surviving. You proved that you have what it takes to stay alive.

THE END

To follow another path, turn to page 229.
To read the conclusion, turn to page 319.

You don't want to waste your signal fire if there's nobody around. You decide to wait until you hear something in the air before you light it.

While you wait, you head out into the jungle to find water. You come upon a small stream, where you fill your water bottle. You can take this water back to camp. There you'll heat it and make it safe to drink. As you head back to camp, you hear a distant buzzing. It's an aircraft! Rescuers are searching for you!

You rush back to where you've prepared your signal fire. Your hands are shaking as you pull the lens from your camera and use it to focus the sun's rays on your tinder. It takes a few moments, but the fire soon begins to burn. The dry wood burns first. But it doesn't release much smoke. You need the wet vegetation to burn.

It seems like you're waiting forever. Your heart is racing. Finally, the green wood starts to burn and smoke. But by the time it does, you don't hear the aircraft anymore.

You tend the fire for the rest of the afternoon, adding wood and vegetation. But you don't hear another plane. You'll try again tomorrow. But you're terrified that you may have missed your only chance. It's going to be a long, lonely night. You know you'll have to keep building fires every day until someone finds you.

THE END

To follow another path, turn to page 229.
To read the conclusion, turn to page 319.

A plane's wreckage may contain items that help in survival.

CHAPTER 4

In Search of Maria

You're alive and safe, but you don't know about Maria. If she's still alive, she's probably hurt and needs your help. Plus a crashed airplane may be easy for rescuers to spot. You might even be able to use its radio to call for help.

You don't know how far away the plane might be. Moving through the thick jungle will be dangerous and slow. But you've got to find Maria and then wait for rescue.

You have an idea of the direction to go, but you're not positive. Ahead of you stands a tall tree. It towers above the rest of the trees in the area. If you climb it, you might get a better idea of which direction to walk.

Turn the page.

But climbing a tree is a risk. Biting bala ants are often in trees, and you could slip and fall. A branch could break from your weight. Suffering any serious injury out here could be a death sentence.

Still the tree looks solid. And you'd hate to head off in the wrong direction.

To take a risk and climb the tree, go to page 287.

To rely on your sense of direction and stay on the ground, turn to page 290.

The jungle is a big place. If your sense of direction is even a little off, you might never find Maria and the plane. In this situation, you feel like you have to take some risks. You set your parachute at the bottom of the tree.

The lower half of the tree is quite solid, and you're a good climber. You don't see any biting ants. You're moving up without much trouble. But as you near the top, the branches are thinner. You slowly inch up the tree, carefully testing each branch to see if it will hold your weight. Snap! A branch breaks and tumbles to the jungle floor below. You catch yourself with your other hand, but the close call sends your heart racing.

Turn the page.

Soon you can climb no higher. You look out and can barely see over the jungle canopy. Far off in the distance, you see a trail of smoke. That has to be the plane! You note the position of the afternoon sun and climb back down. Now you know where to go. You can even see where the jungle thins a bit. You plan your route to avoid the heavy vegetation.

Bala ants will sting to protect their nests.

You start moving. It's hot and humid, and mosquitoes are constantly in your face, but you're making good progress. After a few hours, you reach one of the clearings you spotted from the tree. This looks like a good place to camp for the night. The sun will be setting soon.

To make camp, turn to page 295.

To continue your search through the night, turn to page 299.

It's far too early to be taking a risk such as climbing a tree. Besides, you have an idea of where to go. You head off through the thick vegetation, using a stick to hack at leaves as you move. The growth is so thick in spots that you have to turn around and find another way. At times it seems as if you're making no progress at all.

Soon you come upon a small river. It is shallow, but its water is dark and murky. You could follow it upstream, since it heads in the general direction you're going. But steep banks lie on either side of the river. You'd have to wade through the water to follow it.

You'd make much better progress, but the idea of walking through the murky water is scary. You don't know what's waiting beneath the surface. You imagine caimans with their powerful jaws or an electric eel that could shock you unconscious, causing you to drown.

Your other choices aren't much better. You've been walking through the jungle for hours. You doubt you're much closer to the plane than when you started.

To continue by Land, turn to page 292.

To try traveling by river, turn to page 293.

There's no way you're setting foot in that river. If there are predators around, it could be a death trap. You'll take your chances with the thick jungle.

You move alongside the river, pushing through the brush. After a few hours, you find that the going is easier. You come to a small clearing. The sun is getting low in the sky. Knowing that you have only an hour or two before sunset, you decide to make camp for the night.

*Turn to page **295**.*

At the rate you're going, you'll never reach Maria. It's time to take a risk. Before getting into the water, you find a short, fat log that has fallen to the jungle floor. It will serve as a float in case you find deeper water ahead. You check your pack, take a sip from your water bottle, and head into the water.

The water is surprisingly warm. The current is weak, so moving upstream is fairly easy. As you hoped, you're finally covering some distance. It's not exactly in the direction you want to move, but it's close enough.

As you cling to your log, you start to get an uneasy feeling. The water here is deep. You can't even touch bottom. Suddenly, no more than 25 feet away, you notice a pair of eyes just above the water's surface watching you. It's a huge black caiman!

Turn the page.

To your horror, the eyes slip below the water's surface. A few seconds later, the huge caiman slams its powerful jaws down on your leg. Pain shoots through your entire body. The animal pulls you beneath the water's surface. In your panic, you gasp for air. But all you get is a lungful of murky river water. The caiman is going to win this battle.

THE END

To follow another path, turn to page 229.
To read the conclusion, turn to page 319.

The first thing you need is a fire. You gather dry wood, dead leaves, and pages from your journal, which you use as tinder. You cover the tinder with kindling made up of twigs and small branches. You add bigger sticks and small logs as fuel. Using your camera's lens, you focus the sun's rays on the tinder. Soon you have a roaring fire.

Tinder, kindling, and fuel

Turn the page.

But there's no time to build a shelter before the sun goes down. You sit up all night by your fire. You don't sleep, but at least you're safe.

The next morning you start out again. A morning rain shower allows you to collect water. You use leaves to funnel the water into your water bottle and your mouth. Then you continue along.

You come upon a ridge, which gives you a good view of what's ahead. That's when you see it. There's a black, smoking clearing in the jungle where the airplane went down. You can even see part of the plane. It's not far ahead.

Within a few hours, you reach the crash site. Pieces of the airplane are scattered about, but the cockpit is intact. With a deep breath, you force open the door and step inside.

"Help," whispers a hoarse voice. It's Maria! She's alive!

"I'm here, Maria!" you cry.

You find Maria still in the pilot's seat. She has a wide gash in her head. Her face is crusted with dried blood. One of her arms appears to be broken. Her skin is hot, red, and dry. You think she's dehydrated. She seems to be drifting in and out of consciousness.

"Here," you say. "Drink this."

You help her drink what water you have left, but it's barely a couple of swallows. She needs a lot more than that.

Turn the page.

The cockpit is like a sauna. The metal of the airplane traps the heat, and there's no breeze. You're afraid that Maria might not last much longer in here. But moving someone who has a broken bone or a spinal injury can cause even worse damage.

To move Maria outside to a shady spot, turn to page **301**.

To try to make her more comfortable without moving her, turn to page **305**.

You don't feel like you have the time to waste on making camp and sleeping. The clock is ticking, and you'll keep searching.

The jungle gets dark fast—even before the sun goes down entirely. Soon you can't see more than a few feet in front of you. You trudge through the thick brush. A branch smacks you hard in the face.

"Ouch!" you yelp, trying to hold back tears.

You stumble over roots and fallen logs. Before long you can't even tell which direction you're headed.

As you move slowly though the jungle, you hear flowing water. There must be a river ahead! You move in that direction, picking up your pace.

Turn the page.

You take a step, but there's no ground underneath. The false step sends you head over heels down a steep, rocky bank. It all happens so fast that you don't even have time to scream. Your neck breaks as you hit a shallow rock in the small river below. Your jungle adventure has a terrible ending.

THE END

To follow another path, turn to page 229.
To read the conclusion, turn to page 319.

You've spent enough time in the jungle to recognize heatstroke. Moving someone who is injured is a risk, but leaving Maria in the cockpit would be a death sentence.

Symptoms of Heatstroke

....

- Body temperature of 105 degrees Fahrenheit or higher

- Hot, red, dry skin

- Rapid pulse

- Rapid breathing

- Dizziness

You run out of the cockpit and grab two long, straight tree branches and some vines. You lay the branches on your parachute and use the vines to tie the cloth to the branches, forming a crude stretcher. You then use more vines to tie Maria's body to the stretcher, so she won't fall as you move her. She groans as you move outside but doesn't say anything. You find a shaded spot and lay her down.

"I'll be back," you promise. "I need to find water for us."

You head back into the wreckage of the plane. Maria had a cooler with some snacks and beverages for the flight. As you search, you come across an emergency kit with some flares. You tuck them into your pocket. They might come in handy later.

The cooler is jammed under the pilot's seat. You grab it and rush outside. You take out a bottle of water and give Maria a few drops. She's still not fully conscious, so you are careful not to give her too much.

As evening approaches, Maria begins to come around. She's groggy but is able to talk.

"The airplane's radio is broken, but I might be able to fix it," she says. "I'll try in the morning."

"It's definitely worth a shot," you reply.

You build a fire for the evening, using one of the plane's emergency flares to start it. You find cans of beans in among the plane's supplies and cook them over the fire.

"I'm sure we'll be rescued soon," you tell Maria.

Just then you hear movement in the brush, followed by a loud growl. It's a jaguar!

You could rush into the airplane for protection, but Maria needs help. You're not sure if you'd make it. Maybe you could scare the big cat away instead.

Turn the page.

Jaguars are fast and can swim and climb trees.

304

To help Maria and make a run for it, turn to page **308**.

To try to scare the jaguar away, turn to page **309**.

You don't think moving Maria would be a good idea. Instead you'll try to help her here. First you dig through the supplies scattered throughout the wreckage. You find the cooler Maria kept filled with beverages and snacks. You open a bottle of water and bring it to Maria's lips.

She drinks only a little. She is moaning softly. Despite the intense heat, she's not sweating. That's a problem. Without sweat, her body has no way to cool itself. You pour some water on your T-shirt and dab her face with it, hoping that will help.

As the day drags on, the cockpit gets hotter and hotter. The metal traps the heat. You realize you've made a mistake. You should have moved Maria out of here right away. Maybe there's still time.

Turn the page.

Treatment of heatstroke if emergency medical care isn't immediately available

- Move the person to a shaded, cool area.

- Have the person lie down with his or her feet slightly elevated.

- Remove the person's clothing.

- Wrap the person in a wet cloth or apply wet cloths to the person's neck, armpits, and groin to help reduce his or her body temperature.

- Have the person drink water or another beverage slowly. Do not give him or her beverages that contain alcohol or caffeine.

Maria is unresponsive now. You have to drag her outside. You put her in a shaded spot and fan her with large leaves, hoping to bring down her body temperature. You go back inside to get more water. When you come back out, Maria isn't breathing anymore. You've lost her.

You shed a few tears, but you don't have much time for grieving. Staying alive has to be your only goal. You know a rescue effort must be out by now. If there are aircraft nearby, you have to get their attention.

To try to fix the plane's radio, turn to page 311.

To try building a signal fire, turn to page 314.

There's no way you're staying out here with a jaguar nearby. The cockpit is only about 20 feet away. If you get inside, you'll be safe.

"Come on," you whisper, helping Maria to her feet. She puts an arm around your shoulder so you can support her weight. You start to run.

You're almost to the plane when a huge weight crashes into you from behind. You hear Maria scream as you fall to the ground. You should have known better. Running is the last thing you want to do when a big cat is on the prowl.

Your last thought is of Maria. You hope she makes it out alive. You know you won't.

THE END

To follow another path, turn to page 229.
To read the conclusion, turn to page 319.

You can't outrun a jaguar. And you know that big cats can smell blood and have a natural instinct to chase anything that moves. Your best chance is to scare the jaguar away.

You stand and shout. You wave your arms and shake tree branches. Maria joins in, screaming weakly and beating a stick against the ground. Between the two of you, you make quite a racket.

The strategy works. You don't see or hear any sign of the jaguar again. It seems to have wandered away in search of quieter prey.

With sunset, the wreckage of the airplane has cooled off. It makes a perfect camp for the night. You sleep deeply, feeling safe for the first time since the crash.

Turn the page.

By morning Maria's condition has improved. She's not ready to do any physical work, but she says she can work on the radio while you search for food. When you return with an armful of inga fruits, you find her resting. She's already fixed the radio and called for help. "They'll be here within a few hours," she says, forcing a weak smile.

Your ordeal is almost over. Your quick thinking and courage have gotten you through three days in the jungle. You can hardly wait to tell your friends all about it.

THE END

To follow another path, turn to page 229.
To read the conclusion, turn to page 319.

The plane's radio is your best hope. If you can get it working, rescue teams should be able to find you easily. You head into the cockpit and get to work. You spend hours tinkering with the radio, connecting and reconnecting wires, fiddling with dials, and finally just banging on it. Nothing works. Maybe Maria could have fixed it, but it's beyond your skills. You sigh, realizing that you've wasted most of the day.

A plane's radio may still work, even after a crash.

Turn the page.

The sun is close to setting. You have to gather firewood quickly. As you hack through the heavy vegetation, you feel a sting on your leg. You look down and see a red welt starting to form. Something bit you! You hobble back to camp for a better look. The painful welt is getting bigger. Soon you start to lose feeling in your leg.

You don't know what bit you. It could have been a snake or a venomous bug. Or maybe it was a scorpion sting. Whatever it was, it had strong venom. With each moment you feel worse. Your body feels as if it's on fire. Finally you black out. Your last thought is that you survived the plane crash only to be killed by some tiny jungle creature.

THE END

To follow another path, turn to page 229.
To read the conclusion, turn to page 319.

The sting of some scorpions contains enough venom to kill a person.

The best way to attract attention is lots and lots of smoke. The sun is still fairly high in the sky, so this is a good time to build a signal fire. You choose a spot of cleared-out jungle along the path where the plane came down.

Starting your fire is easy. Maria had a lighter in the plane. You use it to burn the pages from a newspaper she had in her pack. From there, you get the wood burning. You add plenty of branches and small logs, getting a huge flame.

You dig around for damp wood and green plants. They are full of water, which means that they'll release lots of heavy smoke when they burn. As you pile on twigs and leaves, huge plumes of smoke begin to rise above the jungle canopy.

In less than an hour you hear the sound you've been waiting for. It's the thump-thump-thump of spinning helicopter blades. Someone has spotted your signal fire!

Heavy smoke can draw rescuers' attention to hard-to-find places.

Turn the page.

Rescue workers are trained to help in emergency situations.

The rescue helicopter finds an open space to touch down. You rush to meet it. You're filled with relief that you've survived your jungle ordeal.

At the same time, you feel terrible that you weren't able to save Maria. You know that your decision not to get her outside will haunt you for the rest of your life.

THE END

To follow another path, turn to page 229.
To read the conclusion, turn to page 319.

Danger lurks on land and in the water in the Amazon jungle.

CHAPTER 5

Surviving the Jungle

The jungle might seem like a great place for an adventure. But as you've read, it's full of danger. Big predators such as black caimans and jaguars are only the beginning. Insects, spiders, scorpions, snakes, and other crawling things can be even more dangerous. Even microscopic organisms living in jungle waters can be deadly.

Survival in high-stress situations starts in your mind. The most important thing is keeping the will to live. You need to stay calm. Panic leads to bad decisions. When your life is on the line with every choice you make, you need to have a cool, clear thought process. And you must always remain positive. Stay focused on the goals of staying alive and finding help. You can never give up, no matter how grim the situation gets.

Next you have to assess your situation. Are you hurt? Are you in any immediate danger? Are rescuers going to be looking for you? Will they know where to look? These questions will help decide your survival strategy. Do you need to stay put or search for help? Where can you find food, water, and shelter?

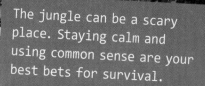

The jungle can be a scary place. Staying calm and using common sense are your best bets for survival.

Many hidden dangers lurk in the water. Building a raft can help keep you safe.

Finding the right answers to these questions can be the difference between life and death. People often have to do difficult things in order to stay alive. Could you eat bugs if you had to? Would you have the courage to climb aboard a log raft on a river filled with dangerous predators? Could you keep going, even when it felt as if there was no hope of rescue?

If you can answer "yes" to all of these questions, you might have what it takes to survive a situation like the one in this book. Of course no one would choose to be alone in the jungle fighting for survival. But it's nice to know that if it ever happened to you, you'd know what to do to give yourself the best possible chance of getting out alive.

REAL SURVIVORS

1944–1972—Nine Japanese soldiers, including Shoichi Yokoi, fled into the jungles of Guam after the Japanese lost a World War II battle to the United States. Yokoi alone survived the final eight years. Yokoi hunted, fished, and gathered fruit. He lived in a cave. He boiled all of his water before drinking it. Yokoi was found in 1972, but even then he resisted being brought back to civilization. He believed that it was dishonorable for a Japanese soldier to be captured, even long after the war ended.

December 1971—Juliane Köpcke, a 17-year-old student, was the only survivor of an airplane crash over the jungle of Peru. Despite falling more than two miles, Köpcke somehow survived with only a broken collarbone, a concussion, and cuts and bruises. But her cuts quickly become infested with maggots and other parasites. She discovered a stream and followed it downstream, remembering the advice her father had once given her. After 10 days, she finally came across a small boat and a hut. She stayed there until lumberjacks found her the next day and were able to get her to safety.

December 1981—A young backpacker named Yossi Ghinsberg was separated from his group in the jungle of Bolivia. Riding a crude log raft down a river, he survived a plummet over a waterfall. For the next three weeks, Ghinsberg struggled to survive and find rescue. He was attacked by termites, survived an encounter with a jaguar, and freed himself from chest-deep quicksand before finally being rescued.

November 2007—Hikers Guilhem Nayral and Loïc Pillois became lost on a hike in the Amazon. They chose to wait for rescue and built a makeshift camp. Their main sources of food during the ordeal included beetles and tarantula spiders. They heard helicopters overhead, but no rescue came. The men stayed there for almost seven weeks before deciding to head out again in search of civilization. On the journey, a venomous spider bit Nayral. He stayed behind to tend to his wound. Pillois went on ahead, found rescue, and came back for Nayral.

August 2008—Hiker Hayden Adcock survived 11 days alone in the jungle of Laos. Adcock was in bad condition when rescuers reached him by helicopter. He had serious infections from drinking impure water. His skin was covered with wounds from flesh-eating lizards. Maggots had burrowed into many of the wounds. Adcock suffered multiple organ failures and was perhaps just hours away from death. With medical care, though, he recovered.

SURVIVAL QUIZ

1. If you run into a jaguar or other big cat, what's the best thing to do?

A. Throw things at it.

B. Stand your ground, wave your arms, and shout.

C. Turn your back, and run as fast as you can.

2. What is the best kind of wood to use for a signal fire?

A. Use only dry wood, which burns quickly.

B. Use a combination of dry wood to burn and wet wood to create smoke.

C. It doesn't matter what kind of wood you use.

3. What is the best way to purify river or stream water for drinking?

A. Use a fire to heat the water.

B. Use a cloth as a filter to remove any parasites.

C. Let it set in a container for several hours until the parasites settle to the bottom.

Answers: B, B, A

AUTHOR BIOGRAPHIES

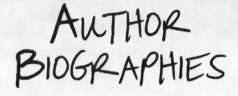

Matt Doeden

Matt Doeden is a freelance author and editor from Minnesota. He's written numerous children's books on sports, music, current events, the military, extreme survival, and much more. His books *Sandy Koufax* (Twenty-First Century Books, 2006) and T*om Brady: Unlikely Champion* (Twenty-First Century Books, 2011) were Junior Library Guild selections. Matt began his career as a sports writer before turning to publishing. He lives in Minnesota with his wife and two children.

Allison Lassieur

Allison Lassieur has written more than 100 books on many topics, including history, biography, science, and current events. She has also written fictional novels and short stories, puzzles, and activities. When she isn't busy writing, Allison enjoys knitting, spinning, and reading good novels. Allison lives in Trenton, Tennessee with her husband, daughter, and a houseful of pets.

Rachael Hanel

Rachael Hanel was born in Minnesota, where she still resides. She's the author of *We'll Be the Last Ones to Let You Down: Memoir of a Gravedigger's Daughter*, and you're likely to find her roaming around cemeteries.